O'REILLY RADAR

Web 2.0
Principles and Best Practices

John Musser

*with Tim O'Reilly
& the O'Reilly Radar Team*

Web 2.0 Principles and Best Practices

by John Musser with Tim O'Reilly and the O'Reilly Radar Team

Copyright © 2007 O'Reilly Media, Inc. All rights reserved.
Printed in the United States of America

Published by O'Reilly Media, Inc., 1005 Gravenstein Highway North, Sebastopol, CA 95472

O'Reilly books may be purchased for educational, business, or sales promotional use. Online editions are also available for most titles (*safari.oreilly.com*). For more information, contact our corporate/institutional sales department: (800) 998-9938 or *corporate@oreilly.com*.

Editor: Simon St.Laurent

Production Editor: Laurel R.T. Ruma

Proofreader: Marlowe Shaeffer

Cover Designers: Steve Fehler and Karen Montgomery

Interior Designer: Ron Bilodeau

Illustrator: Robert Romano

Nutshell Handbook, the Nutshell Handbook logo, and the O'Reilly logo are registered trademarks of O'Reilly Media, Inc.

Many of the designations used by manufacturers and sellers to distinguish their products are claimed as trademarks. Where those designations appear in this report, and O'Reilly Media, Inc. was aware of a trademark claim, the designations have been printed in caps or initial caps.

While every precaution has been taken in the preparation of this report, the publisher and authors assume no responsibility for errors or omissions, or for damages resulting from the use of the information contained herein.

ISBN-10: 0-596-52769-1

ISBN-13: 978-0-596-52769-3

[M]

[5]Benedict Anderson, *Imagined Communities: Reflections of the Origins and Spread of Nationalism* (London: Verso, 1983).

[6]Burton Benedict, "International Exhibitions and National Identity," *Anthropology Today* 7, no. 3 (June 1991): 5. See also Zeynep Celik, *Displaying the Orient: Architecture of Islam at Nineteenth-Century World's Fairs* (Berkeley: University of California Press, 1992) and Paul Greenhalgh, *Ephemeral Vista: The Expositions Universelles, Great Exhibitions, and World's Fairs, 1851-1939* (Manchester: Manchester University Press, 1988).

[7]Eric Hobsbawm, "Introduction: Inventing Traditions," in *The Invention of Tradition*, ed. Eric Hobshawn and Terence Rogers (Cambridge: Cambridge University Press, 1983), 14.

[8]James Baldwin quoted in James B. Haynes, ed. *History of the Trans-Mississippi and International of 1898* (Omaha, NE: Woodward and Tiernan, 1910), 347.

[9]Gurdon Wattles, quoted in Haynes, *History*, 59. Wattles was the president of the board of managers of the Omaha fair. See also Henry Wysham Lanier, "The Great Fair at Omaha," *American Monthly Review of Reviews* 18, no. 1 (July 1898): 53-54, and James Mooney, "The Indian Congress at Omaha," *American Anthropologist* 1, no. 1 (January 1899): 126.

[10]William Allen White, "An Appreciation of the West: Apropos of the Omaha Exposition," *McClure's* 11, no. 6 (October 1898): 576.

[11]Patrice Kay Beam, "The Last Victorian Fair: The Trans-Mississippi Exposition," *Journal of the American West* 33, no. 1 (January 1994): 13.

[12]Lanier, "The Great Fair," 57.

[13]Haynes, *History*, 143. See also Octave Thanet [Alice French], "The Trans-Mississippi Exposition," *Cosmopolitan* 25, no. 6 (October 1898): 610.

[14]The terms *continental* and *imperial frontier* are from Richard Slotkin, "Buffalo Bill's Wild West and the *Mythologization of the American Frontier*," in eds. Amy Kaplan and Donald E. Pease. *Cultures of United States Imperialism* (Durham, NC: Duke University Press, 1993), 179.

[15]Thanet, "Trans-Mississippi Exposition," 608.

[16]Rydell, *All the World's a Fair*, 120. See also Thanet, "Trans-Mississippi Exposition," 608.

[17]For Kipling's poem, see David Traxel, *1898: The Birth of the American Century* (New York: Knopf, 1998), 315. See also Rydell, *All the World's a Fair*, 120.

[18]Thanet, "Trans-Mississippi Exposition," 612.

[19]Rydell, *All the World's a Fair*, 112. For an in-depth discussion of the details and ideological implications of the Indian Congress, see 111-18. See also James Mooney, "The Indian Congress at Omaha," *American Anthropologist* 1, no. 1 (January 1899): 126-49.

[20] *Omaha World Herald*, 8 September 8 1898, cited in Beam, "Last Victorian Fair," 15.

[21]See Thanet, "Trans-Mississippi Exposition," 613, and White, "Appreciation of the West, 578.

[22]Walter L. Williams, "United States Indian Policy and the Debate over Philippine Annexation: Implication for the Origins of American Imperialism," *Journal of American History* 66, no. 4 (March 1980): 810.

[23]For information on the 1899 Greater America Exposition, see Rydell, *All the World's a Fair*, 124-25.

[24]Rydell, *All the World's a Fair*, 124.

[25]Michele H. Bogart, *Public Sculpture and the Civic Ideal in New York City, 1890-1930* (Washington, DC: Smithsonian Institution Press, 1989), 97.

[26]See Walter H. Page, "The Pan-American Exposition," *World's Work* 2, no. 4 (August 1901): 1023. See also Joann Marie Thompson, "The Art and Architecture of the Pan-American Exposition, Buffalo, New York, 1901" (Ph.D. diss., Rutgers University, 1980).

[27]Page, "Pan-American," 1038-39.

[28]Irwin, *The New Niagara*, 166-67. See also David E. Nye, *American Technological Sublime* (Cambridge: MIT Press, 1994).

[29]Irwin, *The New Niagara*, 169-70.

[30]C. Y. Turner, "Organization As Applied to Art," *Cosmopolitan* 31, no. 5 (September 1901): 494-95.

[31]Julian Hawthorne, "Some Novelties at Buffalo Fair," *Cosmopolitan* 31, no. 5 (September 1901): 486. This entire issue of *Cosmopolitan* is devoted to the Pan-American Exposition.

[32]Richard H. Barry, *Snapshots of the Midway of the Pan-American Exposition* (Buffalo, NY: Robert Allen Reid, 1901), 37-42.

[33] Rydell, *All the World's a Fair*, 138-39.

[34] Celik, *Displaying the Orient*, 2

[35] Thompson, "Art and Architecture," 161-81.

[36] Charles H. Caffin, "The Picture Exhibition at the Pan-American Exposition," *International Studio* 14, no. 54 (August 1901): xiii.

[37] For a discussion of this memorial sculpture within the context of racial discourse during the nineteenth century, see Kirk Savage, *Standing Soldier, Kneeling Slaves: Race, War, and Monument in Nineteenth-Century America* (Princeton, NJ: Princeton University Press, 1997), 193-207.

[38] Amy Kaplan, "Black and Blue on San Juan Hill," in Kaplan and Pease, *Cultures of United States Imperialism*, 219.

[39] Page, "Pan-American," 1046-47.

[40] Ibid., 1047.

[41] Nicholas Murray Butler, "The Educational Influence of the Exposition," *Cosmopolitan* 31, no. 5 (September 1901): 540.

[42] Rydell, *All the World's a Fair*, 4

[43] Ibid., 152.

[44] *New York Times,* (6 September 1901), 1.

[45] *Harper's Weekly* 45, no. 2337 (5 October 1901), cover.

[46] Although the Louisiana Purchase Exposition is beyond the scope of this discussion, there is a great deal of literature on the fair. See Rydell, *All the World's a Fair*, 154-83.

Contents

Executive Summary 7

Section I: Market Drivers of Web 2.0 8
    Six Key Market Drivers 8

Section II: Ingredients of Web 2.0 Success 12
    The Eight Core Patterns 12
    Web 2.0 Patterns and Practices Quick Reference 14

Section III: Web 2.0 Exemplars 57
    Web 2.0 Profile: Amazon.com 60
    Web 2.0 Profile: Flickr.com 72

Section IV: Web 2.0 Assessment 80

Appendix A: Web 2.0 Reading List 88

Appendix B: Technologies of Web 2.0 91

Endnotes 94

O'Reilly Media Inc.

Web 2.0 Principles and Best Practices, Fall 2006

Introduction

In 2004, we realized that the Web was on the cusp of a new era, one that would finally let loose the power of network effects, setting off a surge of innovation and opportunity. To help usher in this new era, O'Reilly Media and CMP launched a conference that showcased the innovators who were driving it. When O'Reilly's Dale Dougherty came up with the term "Web 2.0" during a brainstorming session, we knew we had the name for the conference. What we didn't know was that the industry would embrace the Web 2.0 meme and that it would come to represent the new Web.

Web 2.0 is much more than just pasting a new user interface onto an old application. It's a way of thinking, a new perspective on the entire business of software—from concept through delivery, from marketing through support. Web 2.0 thrives on network effects: databases that get richer the more people interact with them, applications that are smarter the more people use them, marketing that is driven by user stories and experiences, and applications that interact with each other to form a broader computing platform.

The trend toward networked applications is accelerating. While Web 2.0 has initially taken hold in consumer-facing applications, the infrastructure required to build these applications, and the scale at which they are operating, means that, much as PCs took over from mainframes in a classic demonstration of Clayton Christensen's "innovator's dilemma" hypothesis, web applications can and will move into the enterprise space.

Two years ago we launched the Web 2.0 Conference to evangelize Web 2.0 and to get the industry to take notice of the seismic shift we were experiencing. This report is for those who are ready to respond to that shift. It digs beneath the hype and buzzwords, and teaches the underlying rules of Web 2.0—what they are, how successful Web 2.0 companies are applying them, and how to apply them to your own business. It's a practical resource that provides essential tools for competing and thriving in today's emerging business world. I hope it inspires you to embrace the Web 2.0 opportunity.

—Tim O'Reilly, Fall 2006

Executive Summary

Web 2.0 is a set of economic, social, and technology trends that collectively form the basis for the next generation of the Internet—a more mature, distinctive medium characterized by user participation, openness, and network effects.

Web 2.0 is here today, yet its vast disruptive impact is just beginning. More than just the latest technology buzzword, it's a transformative force that's propelling companies across all industries toward a new way of doing business. Those who act on the Web 2.0 opportunity stand to gain an early-mover advantage in their markets.

O'Reilly Media has identified eight core patterns that are keys to understanding and navigating the Web 2.0 era. This report details the problems each pattern solves or opportunities it creates, and provides a thorough analysis of market trends, proven best practices, case studies of industry leaders, and tools for hands-on self-assessment. To compete and thrive in today's Web 2.0 world, technology decision-makers—including executives, product strategists, entrepreneurs, and thought leaders—need to act now, before the market settles into a new equilibrium. This report shows you how.

What's causing this change? Consider the following raw demographic and technological drivers:

- One billion people around the globe now have access to the Internet
- Mobile devices outnumber desktop computers by a factor of two
- Nearly 50 percent of all U.S. Internet access is now via always-on broadband connections

Combine drivers with the fundamental laws of social networks and lessons from the Web's first decade, and:

- In the first quarter of 2006, MySpace.com signed up 250,000 new users each day and had the second most Internet traffic
- By the second quarter of 2006, 50 million blogs were created—new ones were added at a rate of two per second
- In 2005, eBay conducted 8 billion API-based web services transactions

These trends manifest themselves under a variety of guises, names, and technologies: social computing, user-generated content, software as a service, podcasting, blogs, and the read–write web. Taken together, they are Web 2.0, the next-generation, user-driven, intelligent web. This report is a guide to understanding the principles of Web 2.0 today, providing you with the information and tools you need to implement Web 2.0 concepts in your own products and organization.

SECTION I

Market Drivers of Web 2.0

Diverse demographic, technological, and economic changes are driving Web 2.0. Underlying them is humanity's fundamental desire to connect, communicate, and participate—motivations that the Internet continues to facilitate in previously unimaginable ways not previously imagined.

Six Key Market Drivers

❶ **Your customer base is truly global:** 1 billion worldwide with Internet access

As of late 2005, more than 1 billion people worldwide have Internet access, and approximately 845 million use it regularly.[1] The overall shift in global demographics means that the U.S. no longer holds the dominant market share, which is now below 25 percent of the online population (see Figure 1).[2] China is coming on strong with a broadband growth rate of 79 percent during the past three years[3]; the world's most popular blog—Xu Jinglei—is a Chinese blog.[4]

Across all countries, the one crucial demographic driving Web 2.0 is the "the digital natives"—those under 30. In the U.S., 88 percent of this group are online and 51 percent contribute content online.[5] Most don't know what the world was like before the Internet, and their complete comfort with the medium greatly influences Web 2.0's evolution.

Impact: The customer base for online applications is substantially larger than just five years ago. Network effects are increasing in importance due to sufficient critical mass. The world is becoming more interconnected, and it is now practical (and possible) to reach global micromarkets. The youth market shows where we are headed.

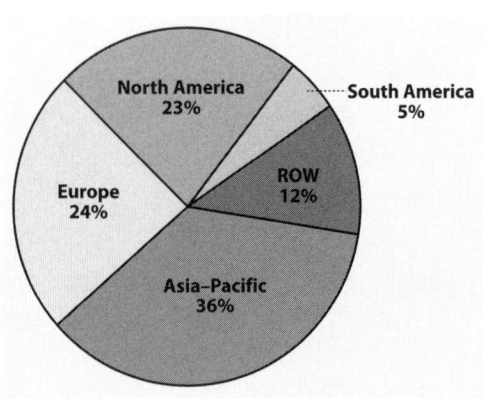

Figure 1: *Global Internet user distribution*

❷ **Your customers are always-on:** Broadband usage approaching 50 percent

We are moving from a "Narrowband Era" to a "Broadband Era." As of March 2006, 42 percent of all Americans have high-speed, continuously connected broadband connections (see Figure 2).[6,7] This is a 40 percent increase in the past year alone.

Impact: Always-on connections make the Internet part of the essential fabric of people's daily lives (53 percent spend more time online after getting broadband[8]). High-speed connectivity is associated with higher levels of user-generated content (73 percent of all users who post content online are those with high-speed connections[9]). Fast upload and download speeds facilitate photo, video, and audio distribution, which allows millions of media consumers to become media publishers.

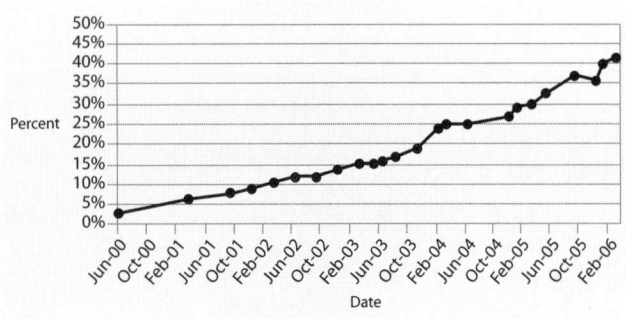

Figure 2: *Home broadband penetration*

❸ Your customers are connected everywhere they go:
2 billion mobile devices

As of the first quarter of 2006, there were 2 billion global mobile phone users[10], twice the size of the PC Internet population. An estimated 28 percent of users have accessed the Internet from their mobile devices (see Figure 3).[11] [12] The rapid growth of more sophisticated devices is accelerating this trend. Mobile Internet use exceeds 50 percent for those users with newer-generation multimedia phones.

Impact: Pervasive Internet access is greatly expanding the reach of the network. There is an increased need for a platform-independent application strategy. Other issues to solve include anywhere data access and data synchronization issues, but there are opportunities for new forms of location-aware applications.

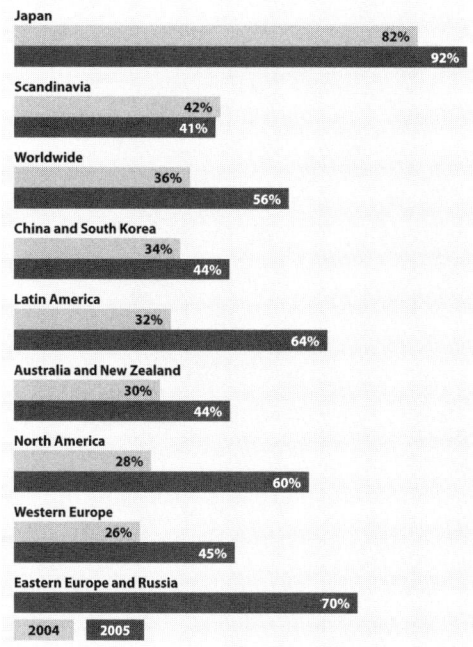

Figure 3: *Internet usage from mobile phones by country*

❹ Your customers aren't just connected, they're engaged:
Nearly 50 percent of U.S. adults have contributed content online[13]

Today's more sophisticated Internet population is becoming increasingly comfortable in creating and contributing their own content online (see Figure 4).[14] [15] This ranges from media content—photos, video, audio—to comments in discussion groups, product reviews, and personal and professional blogs. As of April 2006, there are more than 50 million blogs, a population that has doubled every six months for the past three years, with 175,000 new blogs created every day (see Figure 5).[16]

And it is not just the number of blogs that is exploding. In April 2006 alone the top-10 social-networking sites were visited by nearly 45 percent of all Internet users[17], MySpace.com signed up 280,000 new accounts a day[18], the video sharing site YouTube served 100 million videos a day[19], and users created 6 million new classifieds each month on Craigslist.[20] On an average day, 5 million Americans create content through a blog or comparable means, 4 million share music files on peer-to-peer (P2P) networks, and 3 million use the Internet to rate a person, product, or service.[21]

Impact: The Web is becoming a true two-way, read–write platform. The mass media is being challenged by user-generated content, and these new decentralized means of participation and communication are disrupting established industries.

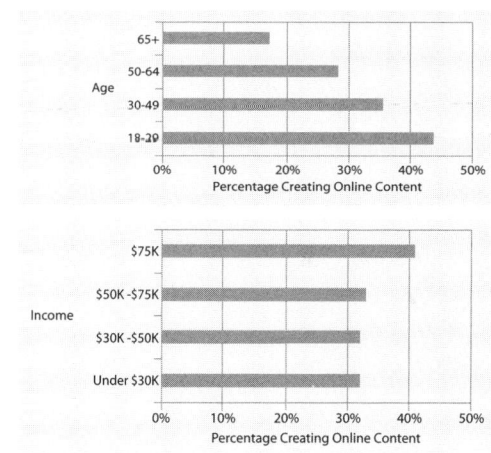

Figure 4: *Online content creation by age and income*

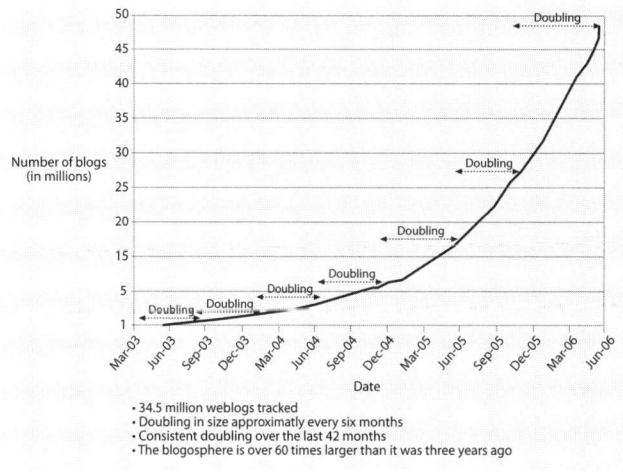

Figure 5: *Growth of blogs*

Section I: Market Drivers of Web 2.0

❺ Your costs of production have dramatically decreased: IT infrastructure costs are down by 72 percent in six years

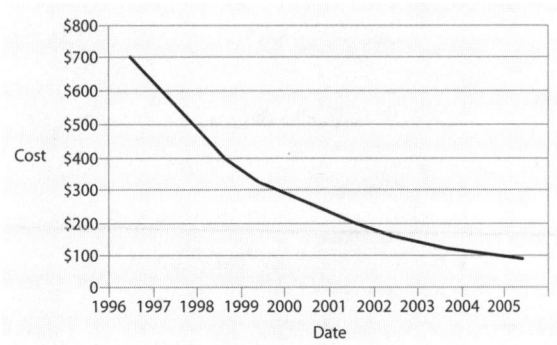

Figure 6: Computer price index

In 2005, successful entrepreneur and founder of Excite.com Joe Kraus argued, "There's never been a better time to be an entrepreneur because it's never been cheaper to be one. Here's one example. Excite took $3 million to get from idea to launch. JotSpot [his new company] took $100,000."[22] This 30x difference he attributes to four factors: cheaper hardware, free software infrastructure based on open source, access to global labor markets, and search engine marketing's (SEM) ability to affordably reach niche, but global, markets.

The Web 1.0 model of high-end Sun, Solaris, and Oracle has been replaced by commodity PCs and an open source software stack. Developers can now run their whole application stack on a desktop, yet that same application in the data center can scale horizontally to serve millions of users (see Figure 6).[23]

Impact: Faster ROI and new opportunities are created. There are lower barriers to product entry. Venture capital requirements for startups are reduced as well as greater business model flexibility.

❻ You have new revenue opportunities: Online advertising in U.S. is up 37 percent in 2006

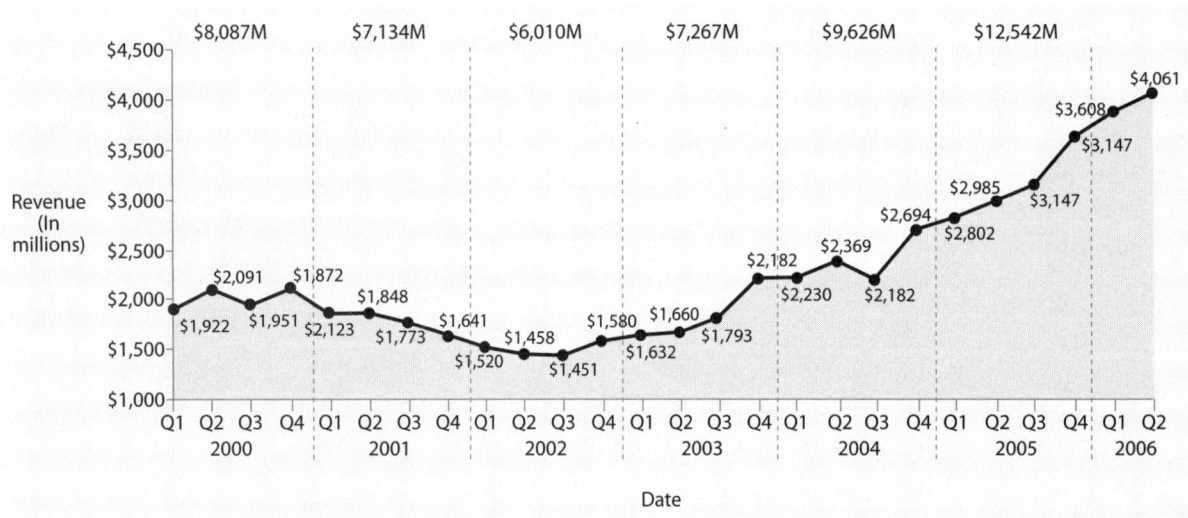

Figure 7: Quarterly advertising revenue growth from 2000–2006

Internet advertising in the U.S. grew by 37 percent in the first six months of 2006 compared to the same period in 2005.[24] It now exceeds business magazine ad spending and is on track to exceed consumer magazine spending in 2006 (see Figure 7).[25]

Impact: There is reduced risk due to broader income alternatives, lower capital requirements and faster time to revenue. Ad-supported delivery models can now support a wider variety of online products and services. There is a fine-grained targeting of micro-markets.

Meta Trend:
How Consumers Are Leading the Way to Enterprise 2.0

In earlier eras, computing innovation was originally driven by investments in the military and enterprise sectors, and later moved into the consumer space. However, we are now seeing consumers leading the way by virtue of their high-performance computers, broadband connections, comfort with the medium, and ready access to powerful online applications. This will reach IT from at least two distinct directions:

- Consumers' experience with Web 2.0-class software is setting the bar of what software can and should be. Consumers are bringing that knowledge, as well as those expectations, into their roles as corporate employees.

- Enterprise software vendors are learning how to effectively incorporate Web 2.0 principles into their product and service offerings.

Web 2.0's inevitable arrival within the enterprise is likely to follow the pattern set by earlier disruptions, such as personal computers or instant messaging, and infiltrate organizations in a decentralized, bottom-up fashion, only to become pervasive and essential.

Impact: Web 2.0 is leading to Enterprise 2.0—CIOs and IT executives will only succeed if they are ahead of the curve through an understanding of the workplace benefits and challenges of Web 2.0. The differences in needs and culture "behind the firewall" mean adapting external models to the appropriate internal ones. Enterprises can learn from consumer Web 2.0 lessons, such as massive scaling, capturing network effects, and creating rich user experiences.

Although each of these trends has impact and meaning unto itself, the truly significant consequence comes from the fact that they are all occurring simultaneously. The most successful Web 2.0 products and companies are capitalizing on:

- **New business models** facilitated by changes in infrastructure costs, the reach of the Long Tail, viral network-driven marketing, and new advertising-based revenue opportunities.

- **New social models** in which user-generated content can be as valuable as traditional media, where social networks form and grow with tremendous speed, where truly global audiences can be reached more easily, and rich media from photos to videos is a part of everyday life online.

- **New technology models** in which software becomes a service; the Internet becomes *the* development platform, where online services and data are mixed and matched; syndication of content becomes glue across the network; and high-speed, ubiquitous access is the norm.

These models are bound together in an era where network effects rapidly drive viral growth, where data rather than function is the core value of applications, and customers now think of applications as services they use, not software they install.

SECTION II

Ingredients of Web 2.0 Success

The breadth and pace of change make succinct definition of Web 2.0 a challenge—one that has led to a lively global debate. The following is our definition:

> *Web 2.0 is a set of social, economic, and technology trends that collectively form the basis for the next generation of the Internet—a more mature, distinct medium characterized by user participation, openness, and network effects.*

Web 2.0 did not materialize overnight. It represents the evolution and maturation of the Internet during the past decade. The Internet, like other new mediums, began by mimicking those that came before, but only time and experience revealed its unique strengths. In many ways, Web 2.0 is a rediscovery or fulfillment of what the Web was intended to be.[26]

The impact of Web 2.0 is now accelerating as the network grows and becomes more ingrained into the daily lives of individuals and organizations. Yet Web 2.0 as a label has become part of the vernacular because it concisely conveys just enough meaning—in particular, that we are entering a distinct new era—to become the basis for this worldwide dialog. The definition of Web 2.0 is a starting point because, in the end, it is the underlying patterns that are much more important than a definition. Understanding these patterns is the key to success in Web 2.0.

The Eight Core Patterns

Harnessing Collective Intelligence
  Create an architecture of participation that uses network effects and algorithms to produce software that gets better the more people use it.

Data Is the Next "Intel Inside"
  Use unique, hard-to-recreate data sources to become the "Intel Inside" for this era in which data has become as important as function.

Innovation in Assembly
  Build platforms to foster innovation in assembly, where remixing of data and services creates new opportunities and markets.

Rich User Experiences
  Go beyond traditional web-page metaphors to deliver rich user experiences combining the best of desktop and online software.

Software Above the Level of a Single Device
  Create software that spans Internet-connected devices and builds on the growing pervasiveness of online experience.

Perpetual Beta
  Move away from old models of software development and adoption in favor of online, continuously updated, software as a service (SaaS) models.

Leveraging the Long Tail
Capture niche markets profitably through the low-cost economics and broad reach enabled by the Internet.

Lightweight Models and Cost-Effective Scalability
Use lightweight business- and software-development models to build products and businesses quickly and cost-effectively.

Although each pattern is unique, they are by no means independent. In fact, they are quite interdependent. A set of common Web 2.0 attributes supports these patterns:

- **Massively connected.** Network effects move us from the one-to-many publishing and communication models of the past into a true web of many-to-many connections. In this era, the edges become as important as the core, and old modes of communication, publishing, distribution, and aggregation become disrupted.

- **Decentralized.** Connectedness also disrupts traditional control and power structures, leading to much greater decentralization. Bottom-up now competes with top-down in everything from global information flow to marketing to new product design. Adoption occurs via pull not push. Systems often grow from the edges in, not from the core out.

- **User focused.** The user is at the center of Web 2.0. Network effects give users unprecedented power for participation, conversation, collaboration, and, ultimately, impact. Consumers have become publishers with greater control, experiences are tailored on the fly for each user, rich interfaces optimize user interactions, users actively shape product direction, and consumers reward companies that treat them well with loyalty and valuable word-of-mouth marketing.

- **Open.** In Web 2.0, openness begins with the foundation of the Internet's open technology standards and rapidly grows into an open ecosystem of loosely coupled applications built on open data, open APIs, and reusable components. And open means more than technology—it means greater transparency in corporate communications, shared intellectual property, and greater visibility into how products are developed.

- **Lightweight.** A "less is more, keep it simple" philosophy permeates Web 2.0: software is designed and built by small teams using agile methods; technology solutions build on simple data formats and protocols; software becomes simple to deploy with light footprint services built on open source software; business focuses on keeping investment and costs low; and marketing uses simple consumer-to-consumer viral techniques.

- **Emergent.** Rather than relying on fully predefined application structures, Web 2.0 structures and behaviors are allowed to emerge over time. A flexible, adaptive strategy permits appropriate solutions to evolve in response to real-world usage; success comes from cooperation, not control.

Web 2.0 Patterns and Practices Quick Reference

Theme	See also/a.k.a.	Exemplars	Practices	Issues
Harnessing Collective Intelligence	• Architecture of participation • Co-creation • Peer production • Wisdom of crowds	• Google • Wikipedia • Flickr • Amazon • del.icio.us	• Pay the user first • Network effects by default • Involve users explicitly and implicitly • Trust your users • Software that improves the more people use it	• Trust • Quality • Walled gardens • Privacy
Data Is the Next "Intel Inside"		• Amazon • eBay • NAVTEQ • Craigslist • Gracenote	• Seek to own a unique source of data • Some rights reserved, not all • Following existing standards • Enhance the core data • Design data for reuse	• Balancing control • Ownership • Copyright
Innovation in Assembly	• Web as platform • Mashups • Remixability • Small pieces loosely joined • Enterprise SOA	• Google Maps • Yahoo! • Amazon • Salesforce.com	• Think platforms, not just applications • Create open APIs • Design for remixability • Build your business model into your API • Be your own platform customer • Granular addressability of content	• Terms of service • Business models
Rich User Experiences	• Rich Internet applications (RIA) • Ajax	• GMail • Google Maps • Netflix	• Combine the best of online and offline applications • Usability and simplicity first • Deep, adaptive personalization	• Overuse • New best practices
Software Above the Level of a Single Device	• Pervasive computing	• iTunes • TiVo • Shozu	• Design across devices, servers, and networks • Use the power of the network to make the edge smarter • Think location aware	• Incompatibilities • Digital rights management (DRM)
Perpetual Beta	• End of the software adoption cycle • Software as a service (SaaS) • Development 2.0	• Google • Flickr • Amazon	• Release early, release often • Invite users as co-developers • Make operations a core competency • Instrument your product • Use dynamic tools and languages	• Quality vs. speed
Leveraging the Long Tail		• Amazon • eBay • Google • Netflix	• Algorithmic data management • Customer self-service • Search, filter, and aggregation	• Filtering noise
Lightweight Models and Cost-Effective Scalability		• 37signals • Digg • Flickr	• Syndicated business models • Scale pricing and revenue models • Outsource non-essential functions	• Sunk by network effects • Defensible business models

The key to competitive advantage in Internet applications is the extent to which users add their own data to what you provide. Therefore, harness collective intelligence by creating an architecture of participation that involves your users both implicitly and explicitly in adding value to your application.

Harnessing Collective Intelligence

Overview: An Architecture of Participation

Web 2.0 reflects the maturation of the Internet as a communications medium, one that is user-centered, decentralized, and collaborative. Succeeding in this era begins with understanding two key principles:

- **Users add value.** Users add value directly through active participation and indirectly as a side-effect of their actions. Users create content, comment, chat, upload, share, recommend, link, aggregate, filter, search, and interact online in myriad other ways. Each of these actions adds value and creates new opportunities.

- **Network effects magnify this value.** Network effects occur when a product or service becomes more valuable as the number of people using it increases. The best-known expression of this phenomenon is Metcalfe's Law, which states that the utility value of networked devices—telephones, faxes, or computers—doesn't just increase linearly but grows proportionally to the square of the number of nodes in the network[27] (see Figure 8). The Internet and many of its most essential applications demonstrate this: email, instant messaging (IM), peer-to-peer networks, newsgroups, blogs, and the Web itself.

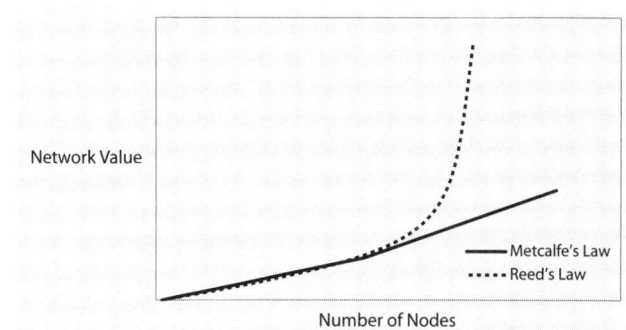

Figure 8: Impact of network effects

Yet the value of applications that facilitate the formation of sub-groups within the network, such as eBay and MySpace, can grow at an even faster, exponential rate of 2^N. This is generally known as Reed's Law.[28] David Reed argues that it's the Internet's "group forming" capabilities that distinguish it as a communications medium.

The best Web 2.0 software is inherently designed to *harness collective intelligence through an architecture of participation*. This is accomplished by actively involving users both explicitly and implicitly, minimizing the barriers to product adoption and use, and by designing products that encourage viral network-driven growth. The end result is that individual users and groups become the engine of better products, rapid growth, and new markets.

Benefits

- Opens opportunities for rapid, large-scale, user-driven growth
- Builds customer trust and loyalty
- Improves products as user base grows

Best Practices

- **Pay the user first.** Web 2.0 products start by *minimizing barriers to adoption* and ensuring that users achieve their primary goals quickly and efficiently—whether it's managing photos, sharing business documents, or booking travel. They never allow second-order benefits, often those related to social network effects, to interfere with the first-order objectives of the customer. Simplicity drives adoption. Look at how the social bookmarking service del.icio.us delivers immediate value: users get a simple, centralized place to keep bookmarks using their own tag-based categorization system. YouTube grew rapidly by making video sharing simple and accessible. In both cases, the second-order value, those benefits derived primarily from network effects (such as collective tagging, viral networking, collaborative filtering, and search) all ask nothing more upfront from the user. The online service Library Thing follows a similar model—first-order value comes from providing a place to easily catalog book collections. Network effects, including recommendations and community, are not allowed to get in the way of this primary goal. The model is successful: within 7 months of launch, more than 30,000 users had cataloged more than 2 million books.

- **Set network effects by default.** A corollary to paying the user first is to set network effects by default—a technique for maximizing the impact of individual user actions when participating within a social network. This best practice can effectively harness collective intelligence as a natural byproduct of users pursuing their own self-interest. In his essay *Cornucopia of the Commons*,[29] Dan Bricklin, inventor of the first spreadsheet VisiCalc, noted that there are three primary ways to create a database:

    — Pay people to do it, e.g., Yahoo!'s directory index

    — Have volunteers do it, e.g., Wikipedia

    — Have it built indirectly as a side-effect of people pursuing their own self-interests, e.g., Napster

    He then demonstrated how this last approach was an essential ingredient to the rapid growth and success of Napster's early peer-to-peer file-sharing application. As files moved around the network, they automatically defaulted to a shared status—not a private one. Due to this one setting, and users' ordinary behavior, the breadth of the data and number of servers in the network grew exponentially. Therefore, to gain the greatest viral impact from your application, ensure that it is designed with network effects "turned on" by default.

Why Set Network Effects by Default?

The need to set network effects by default derives from two basic aspects of human behavior:

- Only a small percentage of users will consciously go to the trouble of adding value to your application. Figure 9 shows that only a small fraction of the more than 1 million registered users on Wikipedia are active contributors.[30]

- By nature, people are inertial and tend to accept the defaults they are given.[31]

You don't need to look further than the recent battle between Google and Microsoft over browser defaults to see the strategic importance of this fact.[32] What this entails will vary according to the nature of each application. A classic example is Flickr's default setting for uploaded photos—public—which is viewable by all. This type of default helped change the entire dynamic of online photo sites from the old generation of private collections to a newer, open model that fosters sharing and rapidly growing communities of interest.

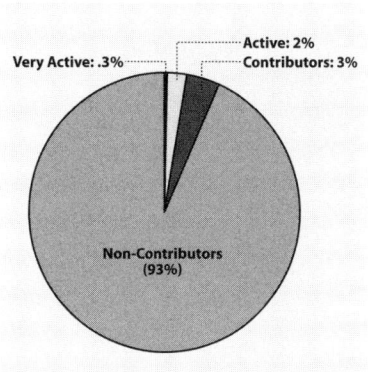

Figure 9: Wikipedia users

- **Involve users explicitly and implicitly.** Maximizing the value of user interactions means leveraging both explicit user participation (such as creating new content, enriching existing content, communicating, and collaborating) and the indirect side-effects of user actions (such where they go, when, how, and what transactions are conducted). Together, a continuum of user involvement is created. The architecture of participation for sites like MySpace, Digg, and Wikipedia are almost entirely focused on facilitating direct, explicit user interactions. Amazon.com's on the other hand is both explicit, through its famous user product reviews, and implicit, via its algorithmic recommendation engine. Google implicitly harnesses collective intelligence through its patented PageRank search algorithms—the insight that the best indicator of a web page's value comes not from the content of the page itself but from the links to it (links that were user-created).

- **Provide a meaningful context for creation.** The most successful architectures of participation do more than invite users to participate; they create a coherent, consistent context (see Figure 10). At a high level, this is subject matter or community context; at a framework level, it includes mechanisms for identity, reputation, relationships among users, data identification (URLs, tags, etc.), findability (user and data search), aggregation, and personalization. Enterprises that fail to provide adequate context are at risk. In 2003, the social networking site Friendster had 20 million users but no message boards, music, or blogging.[33] MySpace came along in July of that year and offered all of these services with ample creative freedom (i.e., trust). By October 2005, MySpace had more than 20 times the traffic volume of Friendster.

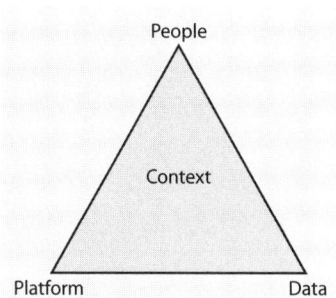

Figure 10: Context for creation

Section II: Ingredients of Web 2.0 Success

- **Trust your users.** A prerequisite to harnessing collective intelligence is providing a sufficiently open context to allow participation, interaction, and transactions. You see it again and again in successful Web 2.0 companies: Amazon.com's user product reviews, Wikipedia's content, and TripAdvisor's travel advice (see Figure 11). In the end, this means the enterprise must cede some control to share control and trust users. This strategy runs contrary to many organizational cultures and is one of the greatest challenges to successful Web 2.0 adoption. But as eBay founder Pierre Omidyar argues "[eBay] taught 150 million people that they can trust a complete stranger."[34] (Note that this does not equate to utopian visions where no controls are needed—eBay invests heavily in fighting abuses to the system.)

Figure 11: Example of an Amazon.com product review

- **Design software so that it improves as more people use it.** By embracing network effects, the best Web 2.0 software (eBay, Craigslist, Skype, del.icio.us, Google PageRank, and Google AdSense) becomes better as more people use it. As the eBay network grows, sellers benefit by having more potential bidders, buyers have greater choice, and all benefit from a greater number of reviews, which leads to more robust reputation management. As more members join, the overall value of the network progressively increases and leads to an incumbent's advantage, both from scale and switching costs. The peer-to-peer Voice over IP (VoIP) network provider Skype, which at its simplest level is a telephone network in software, naturally demonstrates Metcalfe's Law and has increased in value with today's 100 million users. In fact, Skype is so successful that, as of spring 2006, it handled 6.9 billion minutes of calls which represents nearly 7 percent of the world's long-distance calling.[35] The value of Google AdSense, an automated marketplace for matching advertisers and content suppliers, also grows with the size of its network.

- **Facilitate emergence.** It is often surprisingly difficult to predict the best design for a piece of software, the optimal interface, or the ways in which users will use the application. Every software application faces this challenge. Web 2.0 applications impose less upfront structure and minimize the number of hard-wired assumptions to let optimal use and structure emerge over time, based on real-world application and not unreliable predictions. This encourages *unintended uses* and allows user behavior to influence everything from product direction to interface navigation. Entire products can emerge: Flickr began life as an online multiplayer game but over time it became clear that the photo-sharing features were driving interest and traffic. User interface and navigation can emerge: tag clouds begin as a blank slate and take form as users begin assigning tags (user-defined keywords) to content on a site; eventually, the most frequently used tags become a larger font, which facilitates global navigation and search (see Figure 12).

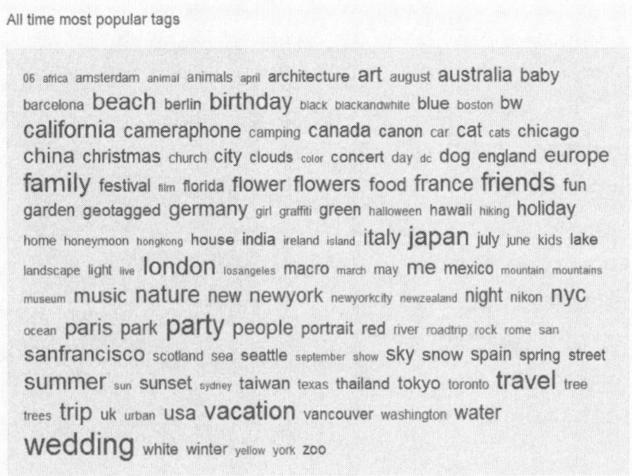

Figure 12: An example of a tag cloud

Folksonomies and the Rise of Tagging

Tagging—individuals using keywords of their own choosing to classify objects online, including photos, bookmarks, products, and blog posts—is common with Web 2.0-style sites. These folksonomies (a neologism derived from "folks" and "taxonomy") provide a number of benefits:

- Hierarchies by definition are top-down and typically defined in a centralized fashion, which is an impractical model poorly suited to the collaborative, decentralized, highly networked world of Web 2.0.

- Rich media, such as audio and video, benefit from this explicit metadata because other forms of extracting meaning and searching is still a challenge.

- Tags facilitate second-order effects by virtue of the aggregate, collective intelligence that can be mined from the data set (enough to overcome differences in individual tag choices for identical items).

Issues & Debates

- **Walled gardens 2.0.** In Web 1.0, America Online (AOL) exemplified the walled garden: users were welcome to create content and community as long as it occurred within the walls of AOL. Arguably, there are now Web 2.0 walled gardens, such as MySpace and LinkedIn, which have vibrant, but—in many ways—closed communities.

- **Privacy and liability for individuals.** People are revealing increasingly more details about themselves online, including likes, dislikes, opinions, personal history, relationships, purchasing history, work history, dating history, and so on. Therefore, it is increasingly being mined by other people, including employers performing background checks, singles investigating upcoming dates, government agencies mining social networking sites,[36] and tax assessors using homeowners' online comments about remodeling upgrades to increase property taxes.[37]

- **Privacy and liability for providers.** Not being sufficiently sensitive to privacy issues can result in legal and public relations disasters. Facebook suffered some high-profile PR fallout when it underestimated the privacy implications of new features deployed in September 2006. Within days, it was forced to retract statements it had made and change service behavior.[38] Or, consider the $1 million fine issued to Xanga by the U.S. Federal Trade Commission for violating the Children's Online Privacy Protection Act (COPPA). Xanga allowed children who identified themselves as under 13 years old to sign-up for accounts, even though the stated policy forbid providing accounts to that age group.[39]

- **Quality, not just quantity, matters.** All users are not created equal nor are their contributions. The most successful Web 2.0 companies have instituted mechanisms to encourage and reward their most valuable members.

It's All About Me: User Rewards and Motivation

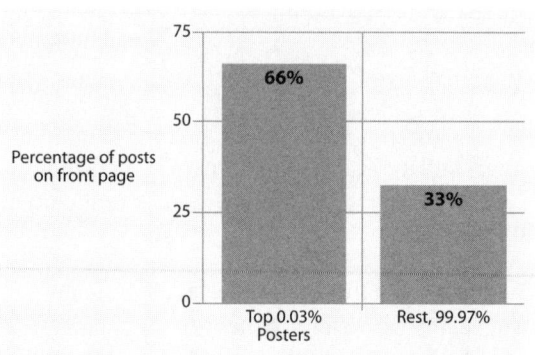

Figure 13: *Most of Digg's posts come from 0.03 percent of users[40]*

User motivations and incentives are occasionally based on money but often build on desire for status, reputation, and attention. These factors become a form of personal currency used for anything from pure ego fulfillment to career advancement (see Figure 13). For example, Amazon.com caters to its Top 500 Reviewers; LinkedIn users gain social value from number of contacts and endorsements; Yelp and del.icio.us note the first to review or link to a site; bloggers want a high Technorati ranking; eBay sellers want a good reputation; HotOrNot users want dates; and Wikipedia offers its most valued editors administrator status with special rights, including the ability to modify the Wikipedia home page. Therefore, it is important to *know what motivates your users.*

Misconceptions

- **An architecture of participation is the same as community.** Google's PageRank search uses an architecture of participation but has no community, whereas Wikipedia has both.

- **Unfettered community, sharing, and participation are always a good thing.** Although it may be true for some scenarios, it is not guaranteed. Depending on the nature of the application and audience, the degree of control needed will vary.

- **Adding feature X makes it Web 2.0.** Creating a blog that is a thinly veiled facade to the PR department, adding tags for the sake of tags, or using a wiki in lieu of a legitimate online help system are all misapplications of an architecture of participation. Beware of Web 2.0 snake oil salesmen.

Enterprise 2.0 Recommendations

- **Leverage Web 2.0's core tools and technologies.** Evaluate using RSS, wikis, blogs, and other collaboration technologies to provide lower-cost, easier-to-adopt, scalable solutions to solve long-standing enterprise issues, such as application backlogs, shelfware, and communication complexity.

- **Facilitate low-cost, emergent collaboration.** Some classes of applications, particularly collaborative ones, may benefit from a strategy of less preimposed structure and more user-driven emergence. The historically low rates of user adoption can potentially increase when enterprise-grade commercial tools like SocialText wikis are used to provide forums for collaboration. These solutions do not have to be completely free form and can integrate with existing tools and infrastructure.

- **Sharing control is key to fostering participation internally.** The architecture of participation is inherently decentralized and bottom-up, a model that runs counter to a top-down, centralized IT control structure. Use strategic pilot programs to test the waters and establish credibility. Ensure there are measurable objectives that align with IT goals.

- **Enterprise has distinct challenges.** Because only a small percentage of users contribute content for most online projects, and even the largest enterprises have only a fraction of the scale of the public Internet, this smaller scale can lead to a much smaller pool of actual participants.

Related Patterns

- **Data Is the Next "Intel Inside".** A successful architecture of participation is the basis for building a valuable database of user-generated and user-enhanced content.

- **Innovation in Assembly.** By providing open APIs, companies such as Amazon, eBay, and Google are enabling an architecture of participation by giving others building blocks.

Data Is the Next "Intel Inside"

For Internet applications, success often comes from data, not just function. Examples range from Google's search database to Amazon.com's product catalog to eBay's auction data and YouTube's video library. Therefore, for competitive advantage, establish a data strategy not just a product strategy.

Overview: New Rules for a Networked, Data-Driven Era

As the market shifts away from desktop applications for individuals and moves to a model of shared online services, it is becoming increasingly less about *function* alone, such as word processing, and more about *data*, including retail catalogs, search databases, auction databases, knowledgebases, encyclopedias, mapping and location data, media collections, and so on. For many online services, *the value is the data*.

And although this new online, data-driven economy relies on open standards—protocols, data formats, software and hardware infrastructure—there are still opportunities for competitive advantage. For example, look back at the desktop era: for more than 15 years, Intel's branding campaign of "Intel Inside" was based on the reality that inside every open system were proprietary, single-source components. Comparing the application stacks from the two eras reveals a common framework but new rules (see Table 1). New competitive advantages lie at the top and bottom layers of the emerging Internet stack. At the top software layer, a lock-in advantage now comes from network effects and using software as a service. At the bottom of the stack, data and the control of data provides the competitive advantage.

Table 1: Comparison of application stacks

	Desktop application stack	Internet application stack
Proprietary software	Lock-in by API (Microsoft and Apple)	Lock-in by network effects and software as a service (e.g., eBay, Google, and Amazon)
Integration of commodity components	Motherboards, disks, and monitors	Linux, Apache, MySQL, and PHP (LAMP)
Single-source lock-in	CPU (Intel)	Data (e.g., NAVTEQ, Network Solutions, AdWords, and CDDB)

There are a variety of proven approaches to maximize strategic value from data (see Table 2):

- **Creation strategies**, such as owning expensive, hard-to-recreate data, or building data from network effects
- **Control strategies** leverage custom file formats or data access mechanisms like registries and directories
- **Framework strategies** focus on classes of data to provide the framework to a wide range of other services, such as location, identity, time, and catalogs
- **Access strategies** provide access to formerly difficult to find data
- **Data infrastructure strategies** provide infrastructure for storing and accessing others' data

---

Five Myths of Web 2.0

Myth 1: It's only about consumer software. Just as microcomputers started outside the enterprise (only to become central to corporate IT) the same is true of Web 2.0. Today's corporate employees are having their technology expectations set not by what they experience at the office, but instead at their powerful home computers, where they have high-speed Internet connections and access to the plethora of sophisticated online applications. This is similar to the way PCs typically infiltrated organizations in a decentralized, ground-up fashion, one department at a time.

Table 2: Data strategies

Class of data and control	Examples
Expensive to create data	NAVTEQ mapping data
Framework data	Location, identity, time (events/calendaring), product index
User-generated data	Flickr photos, eBay auctions, LinkedIn and MySpace profiles
User-enriched (meta) data	del.icio.us bookmark tags, Amazon.com reviews
Enhanced data access	Zillow, ChicagoCrime, Fundrace.org
Control by format	iTunes audio format, KML
Control by namespace	Network Solutions, Gracenote
Data management infrastructure	Photobucket, Limelight Networks

Benefits

- Maximization of data as a strategic asset
- New data-centric business models
- Greater customer loyalty and buy-in via their own data creation
- Data reuse leads to broader market reach
- Value creation possible at multiple data layers

Best Practices

- **Seek to own a unique, hard to recreate source of data.** NAVTEQ is one of the world's leading providers of digital mapping data. Its customers have used this data to build well-known products such as Google Maps, Microsoft Virtual Earth, and AOL MapQuest (see Figure 14). It is no coincidence that its service is branded as "NAVTEQ On Board" (see Figure 15), which sounds a lot like "Intel Inside." NAVTEQ's success in creating a valuable, unique dataset helped it report record revenue in 2006.[41] Although NAVTEQ spent nearly $700 million creating its dataset,[42] many lower-cost mechanisms exist, especially by leveraging network effects through an architecture of participation that lets users build the database: eBay, del.icio.us, Craigslist, YouTube, and MySpace.

    Figure 14: Google uses NAVTEQ technology

    Figure 15: NAVTEQ On Board logo

- **Enhance the core data.** Commodity data does not have to remain a commodity. Amazon.com beat the competition in part by enhancing basic book catalog data in a variety of ways, ranging from user reviews to purchase history. Many of the most successful content and media sites now allow users to enrich data with user comments, tags, or ratings. The del.icio.us service uses tags, descriptions, and aggregate user behavior to enhance previously ordinary browser bookmarks (see Figure 16). Look for ways your organization, customers, or partners can enhance existing or commodity data.

    Figure 16: del.icio.us offers user export

- **Users control their own data.** Give users a means to move their data from your system. This demonstrates to customers that they should *trust* you, and that you have enough confidence in your service to allow users to take their data elsewhere, even though they likely won't have reason to. Just as the reaction to closed, proprietary software gave rise to the open software movement, the response to silos of walled and closed data sources may give rise to an equally influential open data movement.

- **Make some rights reserved, not all.** When benefits come from viral, collective adoption, overly restrictive intellectual property protection can hinder growth. Therefore, ensure that barriers to adoption are low by establishing appropriate intellectual property (IP) and data-ownership guidelines. For example the General Public License (GPL) and Creative Commons models allow IP such as software, data, or media to be shared, but they reserve special rights for the creator. This strategy has been successfully employed at Flickr, where more than 1.5 million photos have been licensed for reuse.[43]

- **Define a data stack strategy.** Understand where your advantages lie within a multitiered value chain of data, e.g., the online mapping space as epitomized

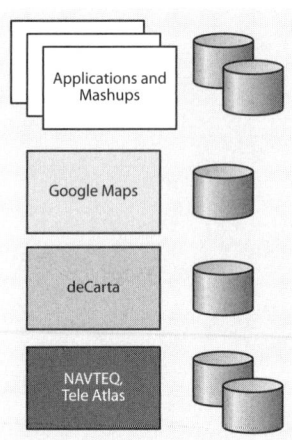

Figure 17: Application data stack

Figure 18: Powered by Gracenote logo

Figure 19: RSS syndication icon

by Google Maps (see Figure 17). Only handful of providers like NAVTEQ and Tele Atlas supply the base digital map data, deCarta then processes and renders the data, then Google applications and servers deliver those to end users, third-party commercial applications (e.g., Platial.com), and mashup developers, each of which can build any number of layers on top.[44] Keep in mind that the boundaries between layers are not fixed—there is a natural tension and competition that occurs among them. So although Google relies on NAVTEQ's data and deCarta's logic, Google has established itself as the external connection point and best-known public brand. Google's success has led deCarta to introduce its own mapping API and promote it directly to developers.[45]

- **Own the index, namespace, or format.** Success does not always require owning the data itself but instead can derive from establishing leadership in locating, ranking, accessing, or formatting that data. One of the best examples is Google's search index—it does not own the pages it ranks but instead owns the best index to the pages. Other indexes and rankings include Technorati's index of blogs, Amazon.com's product rankings, and Alexa's web site rankings. An early example of owning an online registry or namespace is Network Solutions, which rose to success as the official registrar of Internet domain names. But today, LinkedIn wants to be the de facto registry for business profiles; CDDB, the CD database (now Gracenote; see Figure 18), licenses its index of 55 million music tracks to thousands of developers; and Amazon.com's ASIN product index is widely used. Another data strategy is to follow in the steps of Microsoft Office and establish an industry standard file format, such as Apple's ACC music format for iTunes or Google Earth's Keyhole Markup Language for geospatial data.

- **Design data for reuse.** Just as data is becoming as important as function, data reusability is becoming as important as software reusability, and data design is becoming as important as page design. The concept of *reusable data* manifests in data access mechanisms, data design, data presentation, and data licensing. It means following existing standards, like RSS and microformats, making data addressable and searchable, using sufficiently open licensing, and providing the underlying mechanisms for syndication and distribution (see Figure 19).

- **Outsource or supply data access management.** Although storage and bandwidth costs have decreased dramatically, the demands of managing large amounts of data still present challenges. This is particularly true for rich media audio, photo, and video data. As a result, there are new opportunities for providing services that help others address these challenges. For example, 3 of the top 10 photo-sharing sites (as of the second quarter of 2006)—Photobucket.com, ImageShack, and Slide.com—all get more than half of their traffic from MySpace.com, which outsources this function.[46] It is estimated that the content delivery network Limelight Networks generates more than $1 million a month in revenue by providing data management infrastructure for YouTube.[47] VideoEgg provides the video-hosting and -streaming infrastructure for AOL UnCut, Bebo, and dozens of other sites. Using a programmatic approach, Amazon S3 offers a purely API-driven platform for outsourced storage management via a scalable pay-as-you-go model.

Issues & Debates

- **Who owns your data?** In a world of user-generated content this issue cuts both ways: users can and should control their own data, but this is often at odds with the commercial interests of companies whose key assets come from those contributions. It is crucial to establish, from the beginning, content ownership policies. Ensure that intellectual property guidelines are published and policies are in place. Not handling this properly can lead to serious customer relations issues. For example, a loud public outcry forced TextAmerica to reverse course after announcing it would delete data of free customers when it moved to a fee-based model.[48]

- **The cold-start problem.** If the data inside is user-generated, there is a chicken-and-egg condition at start. Some services have been able to seed their initial dataset; for example, Yahoo! Video leveraged its own search data to kick-start this new service. Other companies use a closed beta period as a means to build a sufficient dataset prior to public launch.

- **The open data movement.** Just as closed software applications gave rise to the open source movement, a rise in an open data movement is just starting. Primarily driven in response to walled gardens and the types of data ownership issues previously cited, this movement manifests in open data formats, such as RSS, GeoRSS, and microformats, as well as data access via import, export, and open APIs.

- **Copyright.** Issues surrounding copyright often surface when people are given the ability to share content. Sometimes this takes the form of deliberately sharing material known to be copyrighted—music, videos, and books—even though policy, including what exists on YouTube, states otherwise (often echoing problems from P2P networks like Napster). Other times the boundaries of ownership are pushed, such as when subsets of data are combined from multiple sources, or when layers of rights are involved. For example, the originating source has a license (e.g., a Yahoo! distribution of a Reuters feed) but the derivative work, e.g., a third-party mashup, does not.

Misconceptions

- **Giving customers freedom to leave means they will.** The ultimate manifestation of users owning their own data is the freedom to leave. Mutually beneficial results can occur when users own their data and the provider owns the aggregate—the collective value that is derived from second-order effects: the community and context. This puts the onus on the application provider but, when done properly, it creates an even stronger customer trust and loyalty. For example, even though tools exist to allow Flickr users to export complete photo collections and tags, the quality of the service and strength of the community retain existing customers and, in turn, trust and openness help continue to grow Flickr's market. A key idea here is to look for situations in which the user's data is more valuable in the shared application context than it is elsewhere. Fore example, a del.icio.us bookmark is more valuable than one that the user keeps for herself.

Enterprise 2.0 Recommendations

- **Make enterprise data reusable.** Vast amounts of corporate data are trapped in data silos or applications because corporations did not foresee the potential uses for underlying data. By leveraging simple, open data formats and distribution mechanisms (like RSS) companies can create low-cost mechanisms for wider internal distribution and usage of this data.

Related Patterns

- **Harnessing Collective Intelligence.** Data-driven applications are the foundation for creating an effective architecture of participation.

- **Innovation in Assembly.** Platform solutions and ecosystems exist for the purposes of sharing information.

Innovation in Assembly

A platform beats an application nearly every time. Not only is the Web itself becoming a platform to replace desktop operating systems, individual web sites are becoming platforms and platform components as well. Therefore, consider a platform strategy in addition to an application strategy.

Overview: Online Software As a Remixable, Open Service

In the PC era, Microsoft repeatedly demonstrated the tremendous commercial value of creating not just software applications but software platforms. Windows, Office, Exchange, SQL Server, and most of Microsoft's products formed a proprietary foundation on which entire ecosystems were built.

The advent of Web 2.0 drastically changes the playing field and opens a new era of platform opportunities. Why? First, the shift from proprietary to open standards, a global platform based on the pervasive, mature technology stack of open Internet protocols and standards, such as TCP/IP, HTTP, and XML. Second, the evolution from static web sites to dynamic web sites to today's newest generation of web sites, ones that are not just self-contained destinations but entire platforms—platforms that provide data and services to facilitate entire new ecosystems.

Five Myths of Web 2.0

Myth 2: Web 2.0 is about a specific technology or set of technologies. While there are technologies and techniques—e.g., XML, RSS, and Ajax—that play a fundamental role in supporting the development of Web 2.0, they do just that: they support the bigger picture.

Benefits

- Platforms provide a scalable growth model
- APIs foster third-party innovation
- Open platforms build trust and community
- Customers show you how services are really used
- Revenue models can be directly tied to platform

Best Practices

- **Offer APIs to your service.** Application programming interfaces, APIs, are the core of any software platform strategy. In the desktop era, they typically came from operating system vendors like Microsoft, Apple, and RedHat. In the Web 2.0 era, the APIs now come from Amazon, eBay, and Google. eBay was an early leader in this space in 2000 when it created an API and developers' program to foster an auction tools marketplace. Today, eBay serves more than 2 billion API requests per month, and 47 percent of all auction listings added to eBay are submitted via third-party tools using its own API.[49] E-CRM vendor Salesforce.com now conducts more than 40 percent of all transactions via its external APIs.[50]

- **Design for remixability.** Digital content lends itself to being taken apart and remixed, a principle not lost on forward-looking companies, like Apple, which disrupted the entire music industry by allowing consumers to create personal digital music collections one song at a time. In the past, MapQuest, Microsoft MapPoint, and ESRI were successful closed mapping services. By opening the platform and making it remix- and hacker-friendly, Google Maps changed the rules. Now, the rest of the industry is struggling to catch Google's momentum and the world of web mashups.

What Does It Mean to Design for Remixability?

By designing for remixability, you are making content and information available in the smallest practical unit. The smaller or more granular the unit, the more ways in which it can be used and remixed, e.g., as an individual song, news article, photo, or market report. Consider making your data uniquely addressable. This is the key to creating search and findability for your content. Also, support multiple data formats and delivery mechanisms, including structured data formats like XML, RSS, and JSON, as well as media formats and microformats. New doors open once these pieces are in place, including entry to the new mashup ecosystem.

- **Apply API best practices.** Successful API providers have already established a set of proven techniques to help their services gain traction with users and ultimately establish and grow a viable developer ecosystem. The practices focus on creating a genuine developer support infrastructure that includes forums, mailing lists, and developer-focused blogs; full documentation; sample code in multiple development languages; multiprotocol and data format support; use of developer or application IDs to manage and monitor usage; and a self-service mechanism for sign-up and basic account management.

HousingMaps.com: The First Web Mashup

In early 2005, software engineer Paul Rademacher was searching for an apartment using the Craigslist service but wanted to see where the listings were on a map (see Figure 20). So, he wrote a program that "mashed-up" that real estate data with Google Maps to automatically plot each listing. This application born of necessity demonstrated the potential of what can happen when developers are given (or in this case take) online data and services to remix. It is the Web 2.0 fulfillment of the powerful open source model of "small pieces loosely joined."

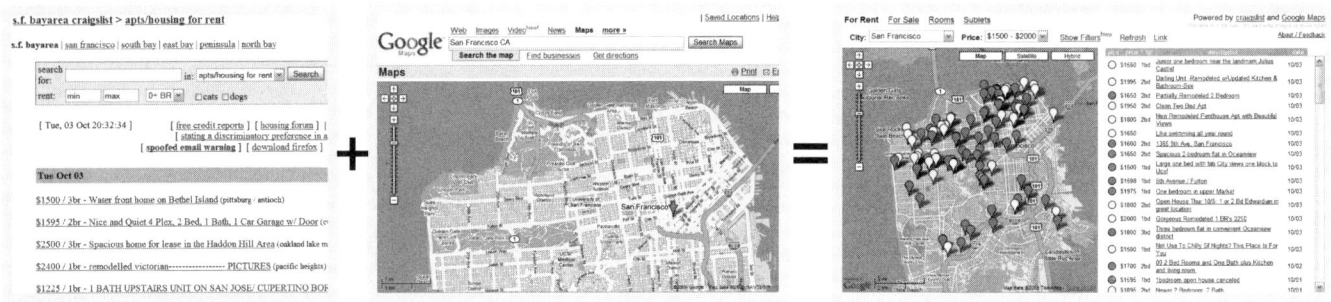

Figure 20: The first web mashup

Note that this occurred before Google Maps had an official API—this was done by reverse engineering Google's service. But rather than shutting down this service, Google instead saw it as an opportunity and opened its API a few months later. Since that time, many of the industry's largest vendors, including Yahoo!, Microsoft, and Google, have introduced dozens of APIs to foster this sort of developer initiative and establish a foothold in the web platform.

- **Use existing standards.** The more standardized ways in which your content is accessible, the more likely it is to be consumed. For example, Yahoo!'s APIs can return data in both XML and JSON formats,[51] the former being useful for server-side applications and the latter for client-side. Google Calendar supports the IETF iCalendar standard. Microformats are becoming increasingly common since they have the advantage of being easy to index and integrate because they can be embedded within standard HTML web pages. For example, Yahoo! Local supports hCalendar, hCard, and hReview formats; EVDB supports them in their events database; and Microsoft's proposed Live Clipboard service will use these formats. And keep in mind that syndication protocols like RSS and Atom are becoming the glue of Web 2.0.

The Mashup Ecosystem

The number of web sites offering APIs is increasing. By the first half of 2006, new, open APIs were being released at a rate of almost one every other day. Developers now have hundreds of online APIs to choose from and an evolving ecosystem of innovative new applications has been built through new combinations of data and APIs from multiple sources. These range from hobbyist experiments to VC-funded and revenue-generating commercial enterprises. The first industry event focused on the topic, Mashup Camp, was held in February 2006 and sold out within weeks of announcement. The ecosystem is in its early days and many areas are in a state of flux: revenue models, data quality, licensing, and technology standardization.

- **Build your business model into your API.** The best platform strategies bake the strengths of their core business into their API so that both provider and third-party interests are aligned in a mutually beneficial way. For example, Amazon.com's API is tied to its affiliate program, which means that every time an API-driven sale occurs, revenue is shared between Amazon.com and the developer. For eBay, this meant focusing its API on efficient placement of listings; now, nearly half eBay's listings come from third-party tools built with its API (see Figure 21).[52]

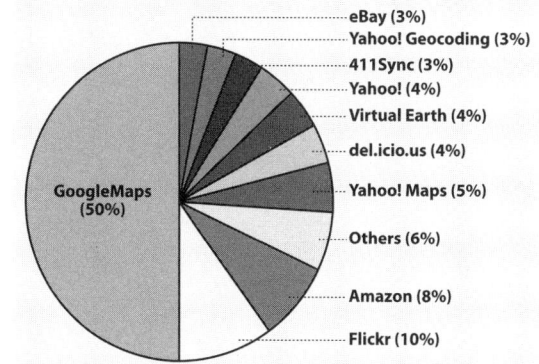

Figure 21: Distribution of APIs used for sample set of 900 mashups

- **Use Web 2.0 to support your platform.** Platforms open the door to a range of opportunities but only succeed when properly supported. Apply Web 2.0 principles like low barriers to adoption and network effects-driven tools and techniques to build and support a vibrant ecosystem. Intuit's QuickBooks uses blogs, forums, and podcasts managed by both staff and users—the staff is the product development team, not support. When Slim Devices, maker of the Squeezebox media player device, saw that customers were hacking and extending its software, it saw an opportunity. Slim Devices created an open developer community resource with nightly builds of its software available for download, a shared wiki for direct employee/customer collaboration, a public bug-reporting form, and even a mechanism for others to localize for those languages built into the product. A planned e-commerce site will sell developer-created add-ons, and the company and developers will share the proceeds.

Web Sites Without Sites

A new generation of web "sites" are beginning to emerge that need almost no site of their own. By leveraging platform components provided by others (like storage and commerce) combined with logic that occurs within the browser context (often Ajax), these sites exist without most or any of the traditional server-side infrastructure. Early examples include Eventsites and the Amazon S3 Ajax Wiki.

- **Be your own platform customer.** This can both increase quality through real-world, close-to-home applications, as well as reduce cost through reuse. A case in point is the events web site Eventful in which nearly all of the production sites are built on top of its own EVDB API. The Yahoo! Tech site, *http://tech.yahoo.com*, leverages its own Yahoo! Shopping APIs.

The Widgetization of the Web

Widgets, also known as gadgets, are small, reusable components that allow content from multiple sources to be easily integrated without programming. Many of the largest online and operating system vendors, including Google, Yahoo!, Microsoft, and Apple, support their own, incompatible form of widgets. The widgets are often part of user-configurable home pages or dashboards (although many types can be included in any web page). These easily-pluggable widgets extend the reach of content and e-commerce providers, social networks, and others by giving users a simple way to build on their data and services.

- **Granular addressability of content.** The web page is no longer the definitive unit of data on the Web—there are also individual blog posts, item elements in an RSS feed, wiki edits or XML nodes returned from online API call. This content represents the future of data access online. The finer the granularity, the greater the findability and remixability. Look at how something as fundamental as a URL structure can be used to expose your logical structure (e.g., *http://www.flickr.com/photos/tags/flowers*). In many ways, this structure has become both a functional command line and a de facto data model that others can build on. And remember: clean URLs for your content—clear, simple, readable—are good for users, outside developers, search engines, and ultimately your own business.

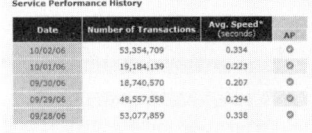

Figure 22: Metrics at trust.salesforce.com

- **Use your platform to build customer trust and loyalty.** As noted earlier, data portability is one of the central issues in this new era. One of the motivations behind creation of the Flickr API was that the founders themselves wouldn't trust a service that prohibited them from taking their data with them. Flickr's API allows access to all this data, and in turn it creates openness and trust with its users. When users "hacked" Google Maps prior to the advent of an official API, the company did not retaliate, but instead opened its system up. By doing this, Google earned valuable user and developer trust. When Salesforce.com suffered a series of outages, it regained the trust of customers by creatomg an uptime dashboard,[53] which provides performance and reliability visibility to existing as well as potential customers (the company went so far as to name the dashboard *http://trust.salesforce.com*) (see Figure 22). Higher transparency and openness are hallmarks of a Web 2.0 perspective.

- **Learn from how your customers remix.** How your customers use and remix your data and services can be a valuable learning tool for your business. As external third-party applications and uses emerge, opportunities are created to tie them back into your product and business strategy. In discussing the mashup ecosystem, Google CEO Eric Schmidt noted "We don't have the resources to build all these. We are critically dependent on the creation of the developer community."[54]

Issues & Debates

- **Terms of service.** The agreements between an API provider and third-party developers have been the subject of some debate because services are often provided "as-is" with few of the guarantees found in traditional service-level agreements (SLAs). As an API consumer, be sure you understand these limits; API providers need to decide what level of support is appropriate.

- **Technology gaps.** Many of today's web services are technologically incomplete solutions with gaps in areas such as transaction support, security, and localization. In addition, few services share data or models in such key areas as identity.

Misconceptions

- **There is no business model for APIs and mashups.** When nearly half of eBay's listings and almost half of Salesforce.com's transactions come from their APIs, it is obvious that APIs can have very clear strategic value.

Enterprise 2.0 Recommendations

- **Start small.** Begin on the simple end of the continuum such as providing syndicated feeds of commonly accessed or updated data.

- **Software as a service, with or without IT.** Departmental managers, tired of waiting for IT project and service backlogs, are more frequently circumventing their IT department by going directly to SaaS vendors to meet technology needs. The project management vendor AtTask estimates that 40 percent of its SaaS business comes from department managers sidestepping their IT department.[55] Therefore, adopt proactive approaches to SaaS and help guide organizational adoption of these new tools.

- **Watch the consumer space.** There are at least two reasons to watch the consumer space: external services can deliver plug-in services for the enterprise, and what starts as consumer services may spawn enterprise offspring. For example, the Google Maps product started in early 2005 as a consumer-oriented service with no support, guarantees, or SLAs. But in spring 2006, the company unveiled Google Maps Enterprise—a licensed, fully supported, more enterprise-friendly offering.

- **Rethinking SOA.** Service oriented architecture (SOA) hasn't solved many of the issues of large fragmented IT infrastructures.[56] Web 2.0 models can lead to faster ROI by emphasizing lighter-weight technologies and development processes.

Related Patterns

- **Lightweight Models and Cost-Effective Scalability.** Look to lightweight technology models such as REST and RSS to reach a wide base cost effectively. Facilitating outside rather than internal feature development by creating a platform can save money and reduce effort.
- **Perpetual Beta.** In particular, operations as a core competency.

Rich User Experiences

The static web page is giving way to a new generation of rich Internet applications that have the ability to combine many of the best elements of the desktop and online user experiences. Therefore, create a richer, more compelling experience to engage users and transition them from a desktop-interface model to an online model.

Overview: Combining the Best of Online and Offline Experiences

Not long ago, there was unmistakable distinction between using a desktop application and a browser-based application: highly interactive, responsive experiences with rich, graphical user interfaces versus coarse page-based interfaces characterized by slow, click-and-wait interactions. This gap has quickly closed with a whole new generation of rich, sophisticated online applications redefining what's possible in the browser.

Combining the best of online and offline experiences creates powerful new opportunities. No longer is a so-called fat-client application necessary to create a compelling user experience and no longer are classic applications such as spreadsheets strictly single-user, single-machine software. Today's new lightweight browser-based applications built using Ajax-style techniques support continuous interactions, drag-and-drop, and full rich media. The result is higher user satisfaction and genuine competitive advantages. Look no further than how Google's sophisticated mail and mapping applications shook-up its respective product spaces or how a new generation of startups, like Writely (acquired by Google), are creating word processors and spreadsheets that go beyond their desktop legacy by adding collaboration and true platform independence.

The implication is substantial: using web-based software no longer means sacrificing the quality of the user experience; now we see the power of data-rich, collaborative, networked applications brought closer to their full potential.

Five Myths of Web 2.0

Myth 3: It's only about user participation. The key to Web 2.0 is not just user participation, it is participation leading to reuse. The Web is now a platform that fosters reuse of data and function on a global scale. For example, blogs have much more impact than earlier generations of user-generated content. RSS technology allows blogs to be syndicated and remixed, permalinking allows more granular addressability, findability—the time element—facilitates distributed conversations, and simplicity in tools and standards makes reuse more practical for users.

Benefits

- Competitive advantages
- Higher user satisfaction rates
- Lower web site abandonment and higher sales conversion rates
- Reduced IT infrastructure and support costs
- Improved performance

Best Practices

- **Combine the best of desktop and online experiences.** Deliver more compelling applications by leveraging the strengths of the desktop (i.e., rich interactivity, high user engagement, and fast performance) with the strengths of the network (i.e., platform independence, ubiquitous access, and collaboration). The online word processor Writely exemplifies how the traditional desktop office of word processing, spreadsheets, and calendars is evolving into the online office (see Figure 23). Users can collaboratively edit documents from any Internet-connected computer using a rich desktop-like graphical user interface. Keep in mind that for some users the most compelling aspect may be the price, which is often free and supported by new SaaS revenue models like advertising. Note, though, that applications like Writeley are not mere desktop application replacements. What makes them as significant as Web 2.0 applications is that their online nature facilitates new possibilities, such as collaborative editing.

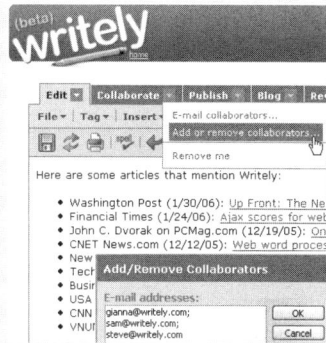

Figure 23: Writely services

- **Usability and simplicity first.** User engagement and efficiency are first-order priorities and should not be sacrificed for the latest technology or interface fad. Do not allow the lure of what is technically possible to compromise the true application objectives. Corporate data-entry applications do not need windows that fade-in but can benefit from data entry optimizations like type-ahead and client-side validation. Web 2.0 applications make simplicity a strategic advantage. For example, in the past, applications relying on digital audio or video, especially user-generated media, struggled with a host of complexities. Startups like YouTube have dramatically simplified the previously complex processes of multimedia with web-based video and audio: it is browser-centric, nearly eliminates file format compatibility issues, makes uploading and downloading simple, and provide easy-to-use, cross-platform Flash-based playback components. Note also that the easy-integration of the playback components have encouraged an innovation in assembly phenomenon, where users readily use them within their own web sites, blogs, and other online applications.

Project Management Simplified

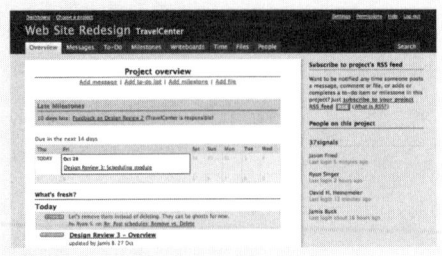

Figure 24: 37signals' Basecamp

37signals' Basecamp service delivers a clean interface and focused simplified functionality that helps redefine online project management, which has led them to 400,000 registered users.[57] In so doing, it captured the Web 2.0 attribute of simplicity (see Figure 24). As founder Jason Fried describes, "Customers ask us, 'How does Basecamp compare with other project-management tools?' We say it does less. Our products do less, and that's why they're successful. People don't want bloated products, and constraints force us to keep our products small, and to keep them valuable."[58]

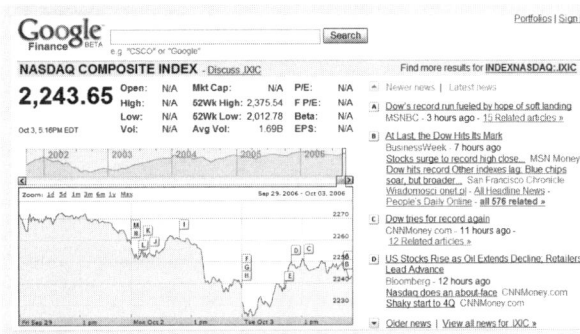

Figure 25: Google Finance

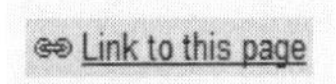

Figure 26: Google's solution to provide a current URL

- **Match the usage to the requirements.** The latest techniques and technologies support a wide spectrum of interaction, possibilities and every application has an appropriate implementation point across this spectrum. For example, Google Finance employs a combination of technologies including JavaScript and Flash to deliver a rich user experience (see Figure 25).

- **Search over structure.** Just as algorithmically driven search engines (Google) are now often more valuable than human-created directories (Yahoo!'s hierarchy), the means of accessing, and even creating, content on individual sites is now typically driven by search and other algorithms. In the Web's earlier days, only the largest sites could afford the time and cost of their own internal search, but now no site can afford not to, especially given that most of the major search engines provide a free, pluggable "search this site widget" that can. The del.icio.us service automatically suggests tags based on a combination of factors, including the content of the URL being bookmarked, your existing tags, and tags from other users. This makes the process faster and easier for the user and creates a more consistent aggregate tag structure for the entire community. As the nature and structure of content becomes less predefined and emerges out of the dynamics of user behavior and participation, the need for smart, powerful algorithms will only increase.

- **Preserve content addressability.** By virtue of creating a more seamless experience without the click-and-load model of older online applications, new Web 2.0 applications are said to leave the page metaphor behind. But in so doing, these rich applications run the risk of forgoing benefits of direct content addressability because one page, or set of information, may no longer equal one URL. Use established techniques to ensure that content is still findable, both by humans (e.g., bookmarks) and by machines (e.g., search engines, aggregators, third-party applications, and other tools). For example, Google Maps allows users to pan and zoom to any location on the earth, but the URL in the browser never updates to reflect changes in location. Unfortunately, this means the content no longer matches the URL. Google's solution is to provide a "Link to this page" button, that when clicked, causes the browser to reload with a URL that precisely identifies that geographic location (see Figure 26).

- **Deep, adaptive personalization.** A Web 2.0 user-centric experience goes much deeper than the surface of the interface—the application's user experience dynamically learns from customer behavior, anticipates needs, remembers preferences, and adapts as appropriate. Amazon, even as one of the Internet's highest volume sites, generates nearly every page at runtime, including what other competitors deliver as static product pages. This enables it to optimize the experience for each user and increases both customer loyalty and revenue opportunities. Google's GMail automatically suggests email addresses based on a user's email history without requiring the user to first add information to an address book.

Web 2.0 vs. Web 1.0: Google Maps vs. MapQuest

Since launching two years ago, Google Maps has had a dramatic impact on the online mapping space. By applying Web 2.0 best practices it has put incumbents like MapQuest on the defensive and playing catch-up. For example, Google was the first to offer a rich interface with near seamless background loading of map data and interactive drag and drop of map image. Contrast this to the conventional model that forces a new page load for each navigation movement. Google Maps was the first to an lightweight interface with navigation controls contained within the map, as well as rich satellite photo imagery and more sophisticated local search integration.

MapQuest did not offer an open, programmable platform until 2006 and is now far behind in mindshare. It is not optimized for mobile devices (but it does offers a premium Map Me service for GPS devices).

Google Maps had 300 percent growth through 2006 with 26 million visitors. This was a rapid gain on MapQuest's 43.5 million users and just 100,000 shy of second place Yahoo!, both of whom had only 20 percent growth during the same period[59] (see Figure 27).

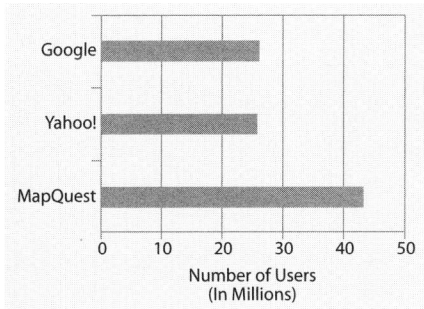
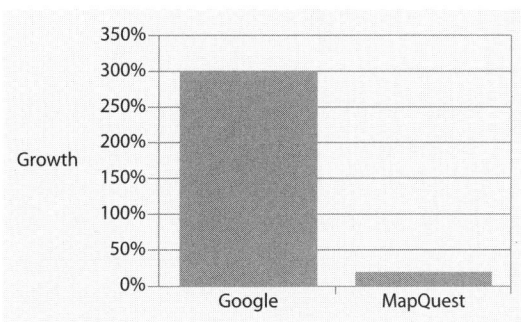

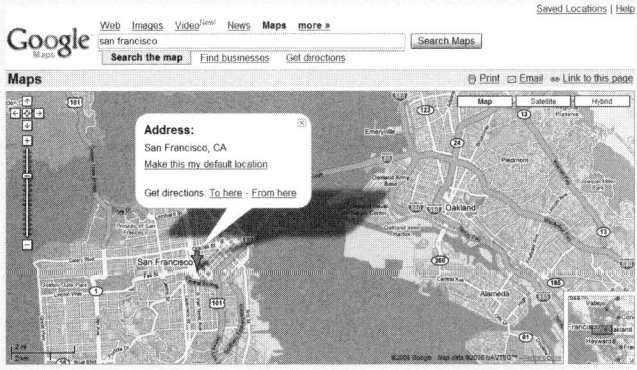
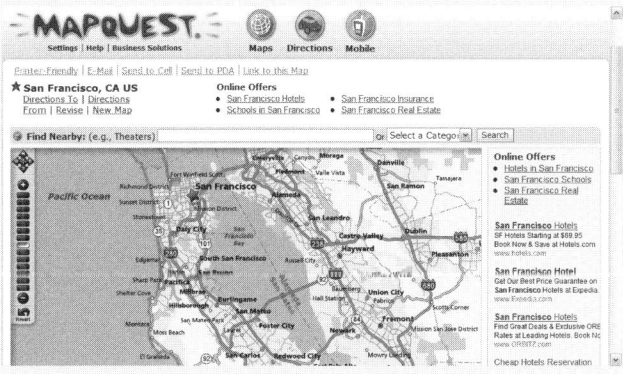

Figure 27: Comparing Google Maps and MapQuest interfaces and usage

Issues & Debates

- **Overuse.** Beware of the "because you can" phenomenon in design and development. Usability and user-centered design should still come first.
- **Compatibility and complexity issues.** Browsers are again becoming a cross-platform issue because complex applications are often not compatible with all browsers (see Figure 28). Technical complexity can increase development and support costs, as well as making top-quality developers hard to find.

Figure 28: Not every browser is compatible with every application

- **Potential performance issues.** Although well-designed rich applications can improve performance by decreasing network traffic and system load, poorly design ones can do just the opposite. Early issues with Microsoft's Live.com product included complaints about sluggish performance.[60]
- **Immaturity and lack of standards.** There are no "Ajax standards" and a proliferation of new toolkits and frameworks introduce design, development, and standardization challenges.
- **Uncertain impact on web analytics and advertising metrics.** New interface techniques have the potential to completely break established models for web site and advertising metrics. What happens to page counts or ad refreshes when the user stays on the same page to perform multiple functions?
- **Disconnected use:** Browser-based applications have yet to fully overcome the challenge of functioning when the computer is offline and without network connectivity.

Misconceptions

- **Ajax is the only option.** There are other technology alternatives for RIAs, including Adobe Flash and OpenLaszlo; future options might include Windows Presentation Foundation/Everywhere. For some specific scenarios, such as rich media audio or video playback, the current leading choice is not Ajax but Flash (for example, videos on YouTube use Flash Video). But, keep in mind, Ajax is quickly becoming the de facto choice for most RIAs, which is leading to a wider array of Ajax technology resources and growing ranks of Ajax developers. Adobe is working hard to counter this trend, and we can continue to expect Flash to be an important player in the RIA space.

Enterprise 2.0 Recommendations

- **Look for measurable benefits.** Benefits of rich user experience are often qualitative—user engagement, customer satisfaction, and product differentiation—but can be quantified. Measurable ROI can come from cost savings at the infrastructure level (bytes transferred, bandwidth consumed, and transmission time), productivity improvements (user task time, wait time, user efficiency, and total steps per task), or in IT support (no install leading to deployment, configuration, and upgrade costs).

- **Seek to standardize.** A variety of new user interface toolkits are now available and most are focused on Ajax techniques. Evaluate these options, including open source libraries (e.g., Prototype, script.aculo.us, and Rico), vendor-provided (e.g., Yahoo! UI Library, Google GWT, and Microsoft ASP.NET AJAX, code-name "Atlas") and commercial (e.g., Nexaweb and TIBCO General Interface). Standardizing is challenging in such a fast-moving, new space. Ensure new standards fit within existing in-house technology standards, languages, and tools.

- **Transition off the desktop strategically.** The trend toward browser-based applications will continue to accelerate, driven by platform neutrality, standardization, and costs savings. Look for opportunities where these trends align with business objectives. RIA technologies don't just replace desktop functionality, but because applications are Net-native, they allow new networked behavior and applications that learn from all connected users.

Related Patterns

- **Lightweight Models and Cost-Effective Scalability.** Thin-client browser-based applications facilitate faster product cycles than desktop solutions.

- **Innovation in Assembly and Perpetual Beta.** Rich user experiences ease the transition from desktop applications to online SaaS models.

The PC is no longer the only access device for Internet applications, and applications that are limited to a single device are less valuable than those that are connected. Therefore, design your application from the start to integrate data and services across desktops, mobile devices, and Internet servers.

Software Above the Level of a Single Device

Overview: Leveraging Pervasiveness

We are entering the era of ubiquitous computing in which billions of devices in all shapes and sizes are connected to the Internet. Soon the PC will no longer be the primary means of accessing the Internet—this is already true in countries like Japan and Korea. It's becoming increasingly common for individuals to go online from several sources every day: office desktop, laptop, home computer, portable media player, game console, and mobile phone. Yet, even that multiaccess scenario will soon seem quaint given the rapid growth of Internet-aware devices and the coming sensor web where data streams online in ever-increasing speed and quantity. This is where the Web as platform truly reaches every edge.

More interactions are spanning both devices and people:

- **Photos.** Snapshots can now be captured from a mobile phone; sent by email over wireless carrier network to a desktop computer for editing; uploaded to an online photo-sharing service; collaborated on by other users via comments, ratings, and groupings; syndicated via RSS and APIs to more devices including a home television via TiVo-like services; and downloaded to handheld photo-capable media player.

- **Music.** Desktop computer users can create music playlists via online databases and download them to portable devices. Actual listening histories are later uploaded from devices to an online music service, and collaborative filters algorithmically combine and filter to create virtual radio stations streamed to browsers and other devices; new Internet-aware home stereo components connect these streams directly to users' living rooms.

However, we are still a long way from a grand vision of seamless anywhere access. Keeping data synchronized and readily available across these platforms is both a tremendous challenge and opportunity. Collaborations need to be consistently device independent. Devices are only gradually becoming location-aware. Many edge platforms have limitations in raw performance, input/output capabilities, and limited or no ability to function when not connected to the network. Successful Web 2.0 applications can leverage this pervasiveness to broaden markets, facilitate new usage scenarios, and gain competitive advantage.

Five Myths of Web 2.0

Myth 4: Web 2.0 is an all-or-nothing proposition. The patterns and best practices of Web 2.0 do not need to be taken as-is or applied only as a group; nor are they a cure-all or silver bullet. An enterprise knowledge management system has different needs than a public photo-sharing site, which, in turn, differs from an online banking system. Although the principles discussed here can be applied across a broad range of situations, the nature and requirements of each application, product, or need should dictate strategy and usage.

Benefits

- Opens new markets
- Access to your applications anywhere
- Ability for location and context awareness
- Entry into the new digital home

Best Practices and Examples

- **Design from the start to share data across devices, servers, and networks.** Pervasive networking has opened new product opportunities for connecting devices and users at the edge to services at the core. Apple's iTunes strategy leverages the strengths of networks, desktops, and portable media devices. This approach, combined with a la carte pricing for music downloads, disrupted the entire music industry. Slim Devices' Squeezebox media server brings the network directly into the living room, eliminating the desktop from the chain altogether. Microsoft's Xbox hardware and Xbox Live online multiplayer service together create a platform with user-generated content, media sharing, ratings, feedback, user profiles, and buddy lists. TiVo's digital video recorder and online subscription service harnesses collective intelligence both implicitly from viewing habits and explicitly via consumer voting. On its web site, a "most popular recordings" feature is constructed based on aggregate user behavior (see Figure 29). The device is programmable from anywhere on the Internet, while the TiVo ToGo service and partnerships with Brightcove, CNet, and Yahoo! brings video to home TV.

- **Think location-aware.** Find opportunities for whole new forms of presence-enabled and location-aware social interaction. Technologies such as Bluetooth and GPS are becoming increasingly common in today's mobile devices, and they are particularly well suited to the digital/mobile generation. Yet advanced location technology is not always necessary for success. The Dodgeball social-networking service facilitates on-the-fly rendezvous coordinated by geographic proximity but because the location data is user-supplied it does not require location-aware devices (see Figure 30). The Plazes service lets people with Wi-Fi-enabled devices at the same location to make contact via their social network (it is also a platform with an API and mashes-up data from Google Maps and Flickr as part of its base offering).

Figure 29: TiVo suggestions

Figure 30: A Dodgeball notification

- **Extend Web 2.0 to devices.** Look for areas in which other Web 2.0 techniques and best practices can be extended to nondesktop devices, whether that's with platforms and mashups, an architecture of participation, or the Long Tail. eBay offers a premium fee wireless service for alerts and bidding (see Figure 31). The Bones in Motion service looks to turn cell phones into fitness accessories in part via Google Maps mashups and instant blog/journal features. EQO Communications and iSkoot extend Skype to mobile devices. Wizbit provides BitTorrent services to mobile phones. Yahoo!'s Go Suite—Go Desktop, Go Mobile, and Go TV—allow access to email, chat, contact, and calendar data from mobile devices and does not require sophisticated hardware or software.

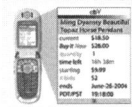

Figure 31: eBay wireless service

- **Use the power of the network to make the edge smarter.** Even though mobile devices are becoming more powerful, the capabilities at the server-side will continue to be even greater. Therefore, offload heavy lifting from edge devices to servers and return lightweight results. With services like SCANBUY and Frucall, shoppers can enter barcodes into a mobile device to receive instant product information and compare prices (eventually these services may allow the phone's camera to scan the barcodes and upload them to servers for interpretation) (see Figure 32).

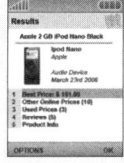

Figure 32: SCANBUY phone barcode input

- **Leverage devices as data and rich media sources.** Use network and media enabled edge devices as low-friction data-capture sources for photos, videos, audio, and text. Mobile blogging (moblog) services like TextAmerica, SixApart's TypePad Mobile, WINKsite, and Nokia Lifeblog provide users with the ability to use mobile devices as tools for content creation and sharing. The podcasting service Odeo allows a user to create podcast recordings directly from her mobile phone.

- **Make one-click peer-production a priority.** Limitations in device input and display make minimizing barriers to use even more critical than on the desktop (limitations differ for everything from mobile phones to TiVo). Apply extra effort on interaction design to optimize customers' ability to use your service. ShoZu's award-winning mobile photo- and video-sharing services focus on ease-of-use as a primary success factor (it also provides this as an open architecture to enable integration with a wide variety of third-party web sites and communities).

- **Enable data location independence.** Allow customers to seamlessly keep data synchronized across devices. Products from companies like Sharpcast and Intellisync allow synchronization across devices (as do Apple's iSync and Microsoft's ActiveSync, although each has a bias toward its own platform). Infrastructure-layer components are also starting to appear, such as Box.net and Amazon S3, which provide APIs to allow third-party programs anywhere-access for data storage and synchronization.

Ecosystems Above a Single Device

In contrast to Apple's single-vendor model for both the hardware and software behind iTunes, some competitors are opting for a different strategy. Real Networks recently announced its Rhapsody DNA initiative: a platform strategy in which Rhapsody-hosted music services are available "in the cloud" through a set of web service APIs. It then becomes a shared data and services platform for hardware partners building portable MP3 players and home stereo components; software providers, including Real Networks, can build desktop, server, and portable applications; and independent developers and hackers are encouraged to create mashups.

Issues & Debates

- **Walled gardens.** The mobile market is one of the strongest bastions of walled gardens. Telecom carriers must first allocate space on their "decks" for features that customers are allowed to access from their phones. New, more open Web 2.0 mobile applications use standard web interfaces to allow access from any browser-capable device.

- **Compatibility issues.** Non-PC devices—anything from phones to media players—use a multitude of standards and device formats. Opt for simplicity and those standards with widest support (such as the XHTML Mobile Profile).

- **Digital rights management.** Now that consumers can access digital media like music and movies from so many different devices, how should content owners control piracy? This question has led to a highly contentious debate and a range of anti-piracy measures with little agreement on what's best to balance the goals of content creators, publishers, and consumers.

Misconceptions

- **It's just about device independence.** Although traditional notions of device independence are important, what really matters in Web 2.0 is leveraging the power of network effects beyond the desktop. Take strategic advantage of the strengths at each layer. Look at iTunes: multimillion song catalogs live on Apple's shared server farms; the desktop browser suits user searching, purchasing, and organizing; and the ultimate destination is the portability of the media player itself. In-between features like playlists and recommendations benefit from the power of network effects and the Long Tail.

- **Recreating the desktop on the device.** Devices are very different from desktops, so design accordingly. Device constraints like small screens, limited keyboards, and processing power require appropriate design. Do not try to map all desktop features onto the device; look for unique capabilities of the device that are lacking from the desktop.

Enterprise 2.0 Recommendations

- **Leverage existing mobile investments.** Every enterprise has existing investments in mobile devices ranging from BlackBerry devices to field service handhelds to smart phones. Many of the applications on these devices are simple client-server applications that fail to truly take advantage of network enablement.

- **Look for a standards-based platform.** Many mobile and edge Web 2.0 applications are designed to work with standards-based technologies such as XHTML. Seek opportunities to rationalize disparate mobile applications onto today's more mature and open technologies, as well as solutions that are not independent on a specific mobile carrier.

Related Patterns

- **Innovation in Assembly.** Software above the level of a single device can be seen as the natural extension of the Web as a platform.

- **Rich User Experiences.** Increasingly sophisticated devices are facilitating richer experiences beyond the desktop.

When devices and programs are connected to the Internet, applications are no longer software artifacts, they are ongoing services. This has significant impact on the entire software development and delivery process. Therefore, don't package up new features into monolithic releases, but instead add features on a regular basis as part of the normal user experience. Engage your users to be real-time testers, and structure the service to reveal how people use your product.

Perpetual Beta

Overview: End of the Software Adoption Cycle

"What version of Google is this?" Millions of customers use Google's software every day yet never have cause to ask this question. Why? Because In the Internet era, users think in terms of services not packaged software, and they expect these services to just be there and to improve over time. No versions, no installations, no upgrades needed. The traditional design-develop-test-ship-install cycle of packaged software is ending. Software has become a service—a service that is always on, always improving (see Figure 33).

Figure 33: Examples of beta services

For development organizations, this shift impacts the entire software development and delivery process. Success now relies on adoption of the perpetual beta development model in which software is continuously refined and improved, users become co-developers, and operations—the daily care and feeding of online services—become a core competency. It is Web Development 2.0.

Benefits

- Faster time to market
- Reduced risk
- Closer relationship with customers
- Real-time data to make quantifiable decisions
- Increased responsiveness

Best Practices

- **Release early and release often.** This edict of the open source development model[61] is now a critical success factor for Internet-based software. Use agile and iterative development methodologies to package bug fixes and enhancements into incremental releases that respond to user feedback. Use automated testing and a rigorous build and deploy process to streamline QA and release management. eBay deploys a new version of its service approximately every two weeks. Flickr photo-sharing service took this even further, deploying hundreds of incremental releases during an 18 month period from February 2004 through August 2005. Compare this with the traditional product release cycle as exemplified by Microsoft Windows (see Figure 34).

  It's not just new products that can benefit from this approach: Yahoo! Messenger went from 1 release every 18 months to 4 releases per year.[62]

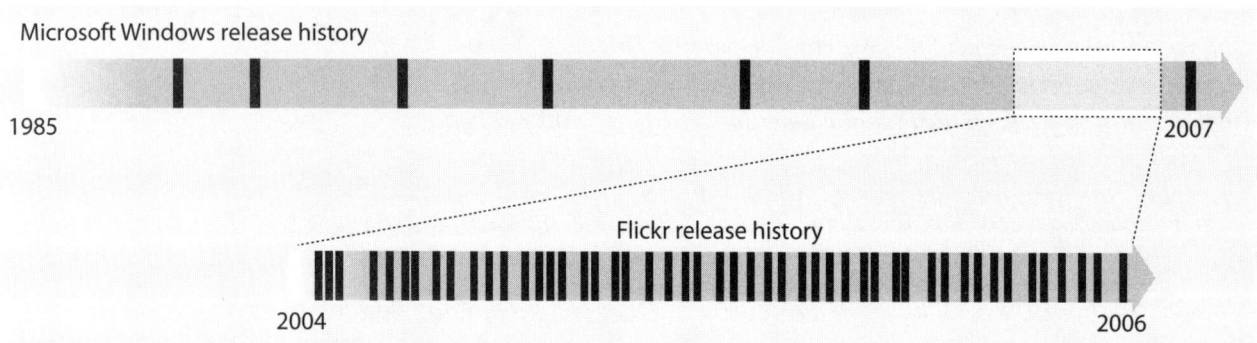

Figure 34: Flickr versus Microsoft release cycles

- **Engage users as co-developers and real-time testers.** Real-world user behavior provides a much more accurate model for assessing new product features than marketing requirements documents, prototypes, or any other form of non-production feedback. The nature of web-based applications and the creator's ability to actively monitor how the software is used in the wild is a dramatic shift from the days of desktop software. Use statistics and controlled experimentation to make informed product decisions. Establish feedback models such as dynamic A/B testing in which a small percentage of your site visitors are presented with alternative features and experiences. Amazon.com runs multiple A/B feature tests on its live site every day. The results of these tests feed a rigorous data-driven process that spurs evolution of not only the application but the business as well.

- **Instrument your product.** In the development process, you need to plan for and implement not only the customer-facing application but also a framework for capturing how customers are using your product. What users do often tells you more than what they say. This framework of instrumentation must be guided by business objectives and be as carefully planned for and thought through as the product itself. As with A/B testing, the data captured must answer specific questions as a means for measuring how well objectives are being met and driving product development (see Figure 35).

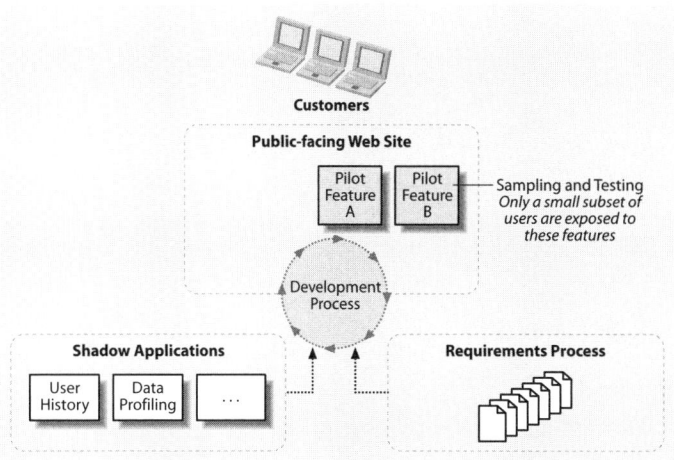

Figure 35: Perpetual beta product cycle

Shadow Applications

Shadow applications are private, internal-facing tools built to monitor and profile public-facing applications. They spot what is or isn't succeeding and ultimately drive improvements. Shadow apps don't have to be large, just meaningful. For example, Flickr developed a "Loneliest Users" report that allowed it to identify users who were not inviting friends to the service. Flickr then added itself as a contact for those users and taught them how to make better use of the service.

- **Incrementally create new products.** New and existing products should evolve through rapid releases, user feedback, and instrumentation. Experiment with new product ideas through planned, but incremental processes. Google has launched some of its most successful products including Google Maps and GMail following this approach. The Google Maps beta was publicly launched in February 2005 and stayed in beta for eight months. During that time, Google gained significant feedback from users, incrementally added new features, and gained valuable early-mover advantage, which put it far ahead of slower competitors like Microsoft and Yahoo! (see Figure 36).

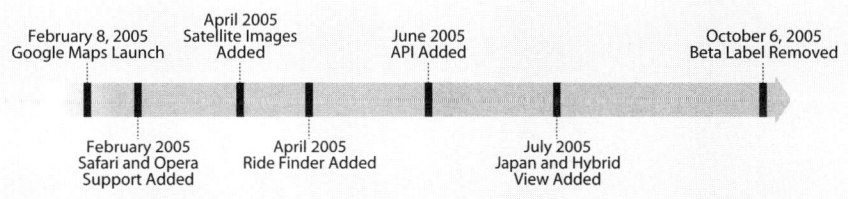

Figure 36: Google Maps beta timeline

- **Make operations a core competency.** When software is an always-available online service, it is no longer just software development that determines success, it's operations—that day-to-day ongoing management of data and services. Google's success is due not just to its patented PageRank search algorithms but how well it builds and runs its data centers. Doing this well creates competitive significant cost and quality advantages. These operational strategies and competencies include:

    — Using horizontal scaling techniques and commodity hardware components for simplified fault-tolerance and high availability

    — Using low-cost software (typically open source) to leverage large support communities and resources

    — Ensuring that adequate systems monitoring and management is in place

    — Ensuring that operations planning and staffing are first-class priorities

    — Feeding lessons learned from operational experience back into the core product—features, stability, and scalability

    At an application level, this means no longer having the development team throwing it "over the wall" to operations and forgetting about it—they must actively integrate deployment, data management, feedback loops, and metrics.

- **Use dynamic tools and languages.** Rapid release cycles and agile, responsive development models benefit from appropriately flexible development tools and languages. Employ platform-independent, dynamic languages such as Python, PHP, and Ruby to enable adaptability to change, speed, and productivity. Consider development frameworks that focus on simplification and productivity, such as Ruby on Rails (initially created as part of 37signals' Basecamp and later released as open source) or Django for Python (developed as part of the project Ellington and also released as open source code). 37signals often notes how the strengths of the Ruby programming language helped enable it to build Basecamp in four months with a team of 2.5 people.[63]

Misconceptions

- **User testing replaces quality assurance.** Do not use the perpetual beta as an excuse for poor quality, stability, or a lack of accountability. This risks alienating and losing valuable customers. Engaging users as real-time testers is about validating and refining functionality, not quality.

- **Versions no longer exist.** Users may no longer be aware of versions but underneath the covers they are as vital as ever. Some companies with extremely short development cycles "ship timestamps, not versions," yet source code control is used for both. Development tools need to support high-quality rapid software development; the more frequent release cycles require disciplined build, deployment, and support processes.

Issues & Debates

- **Beware of excess.** Just because you can quickly deliver new features to users does not mean you should. Avoid creating confusion or feature fatigue with your customers.

- **Beware of release thrashing.** Rapid release cycles quickly become counter-productive and inefficient if not supported by appropriate internal tools and processes.

- **Uptime is not cheap or easy.** Do not underestimate the cost and effort necessary to achieve high levels of service availability (e.g., "five nines"). As seen with Salesforce.com's high-profile reliability issues,[64] any service-quality failures can lead to customer- and public-relations challenges. Because every application has its own level of criticality—an air traffic control system and an in-house collaboration tool are quite different—so look to match service-level requirements to needs.

- **Privacy.** Instrumentation of applications and profiling user behavior must be done within appropriate privacy and security guidelines.

- **First impressions.** There is always tension between the desire to release a product early and the reality of making a good first impression. This requires rigorous focus on feature prioritization—understanding what's most important—as well as ensuring that what is released is adequately functional and reliable.

Enterprise 2.0 Recommendations

- **Seek suitable enterprise process models.** Look for development and operational models that suit your organization's culture but move toward the perpetual beta. On the development side use agile, iterative approaches. On the operations side, consider best practice-centered models, such as the IT Infrastructure Library (ITIL).[65]

- **Start with pilot projects.** As with any new approach, begin with select projects and teams to learn adoption processes.

Related Patterns

- **Lightweight Models and Cost-Effective Scalability.** Agile software-development techniques are ideally suited to support rapid release cycles, so they have a readiness for change. Integrate lightweight development and deployment processes as complements to the perpetual beta. Combine this with low-cost, commodity components to build a scalable, fault-tolerant operational base.

- **Innovation in Assembly.** The perpetual beta is the process underlying the development of the web platform and it relies on many of the same core competencies.

Leveraging the Long Tail

Small sites make up the bulk of the Internet's content; narrow niches make up the bulk of the Internet's possible applications. Therefore, use the reach of the Internet to monetize markets previously too small to profitably capture. Reach out to the edges and not just the center; reach out to the Long Tail and not just the head.

Overview: The Web Has No Shelf

An entire class of opportunities now exists that weren't previously practical. These opportunities are captured in Chris Anderson's economic model of the Long Tail.[66] It demonstrates the shift from a world of limited choices and mass market hits to a world of nearly limitless choices and niche markets. And it's the Internet, with its low cost of production and distribution combined with infinite shelf space, that is driving this change.

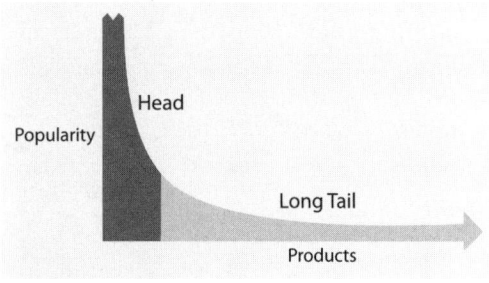

Figure 37: *The Long Tail model*

The Long Tail phenomenon is a type of "power law" statistical distribution often seen in the relationship between product popularity and product choice, as shown in Figure 37. The section on the left represents the most popular products—hits and mass market items at the "head" of the demand curve, where a limited number of items sell in large volumes. A steep slope quickly leads into the much broader part of the market, the Long Tail itself. In this section, each item sells far fewer units than the hits, but the total number of niches in the tail represents significant market opportunities.

Five Myths of Web 2.0

Myth 5: Web 2.0 is over. Some mistakenly may think that this era is already over and that it is too late to take advantage of these changes. However, this phase of the Internet's evolution has just begun, and while the incumbents in some markets may have a lead, that does not mean the battle is over. The fundamentals that are driving this change are independent of the hype over the rapid success and proliferation of Web 2.0 companies that have yet to demonstrate staying power.

What makes the Internet uniquely suited to leveraging the Long Tail?

- **Infinite shelf space.** Many limiting factors from the physical world are absent from the Internet, including shelf space, fixed geographic location, and spectrum on the broadcast airwaves.

- **Micro-markets.** Small sites make up the bulk of the Internet and narrow niches constitute the majority of the Internet's possible applications and audience.

- **Cost advantages.** The nature of online commerce can significantly lower distribution, inventory, and sales costs.

Some Long Tail examples include[67]:

- Netflix rents 35,000 to 40,000 unique DVD titles every day. That's 66 percent of its entire inventory of 60,000 selections. Yet the average Blockbuster retail location stocks less than 3,000 DVDs.

- Rhapsody has found that the majority of titles it delivers are not from its top 10,000 songs.

- Google's automated, decentralized advertising mechanisms have enabled hundreds of thousands of small publishers to earn revenue from advertising.

Benefits

- Ability to target and capture new micro-markets
- Content producers can reach a wider audience
- Opportunity for increased consumer choice

Best Practices

- **Build on the driving forces of the Long Tail.** The Long Tail is driven by three forces: democratized tools of production, decreased cost of consumption by virtue of democratized distribution, and new forms of connecting supply and demand. The new tools of production in the hands of millions of consumers (now producers) make the Long Tail longer; new forms of distribution like the Internet make the tail fatter (greater liquidity and consumption); and better marketplace matchmaking drives business from hits to niches (via search and filtering) (see Table 3).[68]

Table 3: Building on the Long Tail

Force	Business	Example
Democratize production	Long Tail toolmakers, producers	Digital video cameras, desktop music- and video-editing software, and blogging tools
Democratize distribution	Long Tail aggregators	Physical goods: Amazon.com and eBay Digital goods: iTunes and iFilm Advertising/services: Google and Craigslist Information: Google and Wikipedia Communities: MySpace and Bloglines
Connect supply and demand	Long Tail filters	Google, blogs, Rhapsody recommendations, and best-seller lists

The need for all of these capabilities will only continue to grow; as venture capitalist David Hornik notes, "The real money [in the Long Tail] is in aggregation and filtering, and those will continue to be interesting businesses for the foreseeable future."[69]

- **Use algorithmic data management to match supply and demand.** The now familiar online retail refrain "Customers who bought this also bought X" epitomizes application of algorithmic techniques to help consumers find products of similar interest. As the number of available products swells, this type of behind the scenes collaborative filtering, pioneered by early online retailers including Amazon.com, becomes even more critical.

Google's Mission: Serving the Long Tail

There is a Long Tail for search technology, and it was Google, not Excite, that found a way to monetize it with automated, efficient, highly targeted advertising. Google's self-service model allows both advertisers and publishers to manage the entire process. Google targets the Long Tail in its role of aggregator: search is a form of aggregation, and as it moves into verticals—e.g., video, local, and news—Google can feed more niches. As CEO Eric Schmidt put it, Google's mission is "serving the Long Tail."

- **Use an architecture of participation to match supply and demand.** An open architecture of participation can fulfill a powerful complementary role to algorithmic techniques to more effectively feed niches. James Surowiecki's "wisdom of crowds" philosophy"[70] is being leveraged by companies and products of all types as a means for searching and filtering the Long Tail. Capitalizing on the wisdom of crowds extends from user product reviews to popularity rankings and other aggregated wisdom. This now fulfills a need that extends far beyond retail. For example, the *New York Times* web site now offers live rankings of "most popular" and "most emailed" as filters to dynamically prioritize content based on user behavior.

Controlling the Wisdom of Crowds

Just as email begat spam, and bulletin boards bred trolls and flamers, the latest generation of Internet technologies, including blogs, wikis, and every web site that is now "read–write" and not just "read" must confront new variations of the same challenges: preventing or filtering fraudulent, obscene, illegal, and otherwise inappropriate material.

As you open your application to outside input, it is vital to plan and prepare for this inevitability. Fortunately, there are a variety of techniques available for controlling the wisdom of crowds, including both algorithmic software-only solutions and manual human-controlled approaches. These can be applied individually or in combination depending on need. Consider:

- **Captchas:** A verification technique to prevent abuse by robots and other automated spam software. Typically it presents the user with an image containing distorted text and asks him to confirm its contents; e.g., Yahoo! account signup (see Figure 38).[71]

- **Editorial review:** Content reviewed and approved by the editorial team or editorial hierarchy; e.g., Wikipedia.

Figure 38: An example of a Captcha

- **User moderation:** Content moderation via fellow users ranging from rating systems open to all users or to control by delegated moderators; e.g., Slashdot's "mod points" system.

- **Abuse reporting:** Allows fellow users to report specific instances of abuse through a generalized report abuse form or flag presented alongside each content element; e.g., Amazon.com's Report Abuse flags for user reviews, Craigslist's "flag for review," and YouTube's "flag as inappropriate" feature.

- **Reputation systems:** Mechanism for scoring or rating fellow users. Users with low scores can be blocked or avoided; e.g., eBay.

- **Algorithmic spam detection:** Software that scans content for potential abuse patterns; it can automatically remove content or flag and forward for human moderation; e.g., Spam Karma for WordPress.

- **Relevance ranking:** Algorithmic ranking that either filters inappropriate content or mitigates its effectiveness; e.g., Google Search.

These mechanisms are also a means for protecting and reinforcing the essential Web 2.0 element of trust: trust in the quality of data, trust in the system, and trust between other users.

- **Leverage customer self-service to cost effectively reach the entire web.** Allowing customers to manage their own accounts gives them greater control and information, while simultaneously reducing total support costs, which is one of the greatest barriers to scalable growth. Nearly all of Google's services are self-service based. Skype, eBay, and Craigslist all succeeded on self-service models. The same strategy can be applied to business and enterprise customers: Microsoft's new Office Live SaaS product line follows a self-service model that allows it to reach the large, but cost-sensitive, Long Tail of the small- to medium-size business (SMB) market.

- **Leverage the low-cost advantages of being online.** Production and inventory costs can be kept low by fulfilling an aggregation role (e.g., eBay and iFilm) by using consignment-style models (Apple pays for iTunes tracks only after they are sold) and build-on-demand (e.g., on-demand books through lulu.com or Amazon.com's BookSurge and DVDs-to-order through CustomFlix). Minimizing marketing costs comes from customer driven word-of-mouth promotion, and reducing support and training costs via self-service and community support (e.g., forums, groups, and wikis).

Issues & Debates

- **Some markets and goods benefit more.** Digital goods, with their low (near-zero) cost of production and distribution, are particularly well suited to leverage the Long Tail.

- **When the tail is smaller.** Size matters for Long Tail markets. But some contexts, such as within a single enterprise, have in inherently smaller population than the global Internet. These smaller populations require finding the right incentives and means for demonstrating and reinforcing value.

Misconceptions

- **Hits don't matter.** Hits do matter, but go beyond their traditional role by serving as the launching point from which techniques like recommendations and rankings can lead customers into more specialized and personalized areas of interest. Even in new markets, the head of the curve still matters. For example, YouTube's top 10 percent of best-played videos made up 79 percent of all of its 7.56 billion plays.[72]

Enterprise 2.0 Recommendations

- **Enable enterprise self-service.** Reduce costs and address IT's Long Tail demand by enabling more self-service IT with tools like wikis and mashup-style integration tools (considered supported tools from vendors such as Socialtext, Confluence for collaboration, or Kapow Technologies and Zimba for integration).

- **Improve search, filtering, and aggregation.** Effective information retrieval of both structured and unstructured enterprise data is one of corporate IT's greatest deficiencies—this is where vast amounts of valuable information goes underused. Look for opportunities to apply these core Long Tail techniques to match this supply of data with user demand.

Related Patterns

- **Lightweight Models and Cost-Effective Scalability.** Gain Long Tail-style benefits with syndicated business models and maintained low costs. Scalable, elastic pricing models allow pricing to match more markets.

- **Data Is the Next "Intel Inside".** Making data (content) accessible to niches means making it available in smaller "micro" chunks. iTunes sells music by the song, not the CD, and newspapers like the *New York Times* sell individual articles online.

- **Harnessing Collective Intelligence.** Using peer production and other "crowdsourcing" techniques to capture the Long Tail.

Lightweight Models and Cost-Effective Scalability

Scalability in Web 2.0 applies to business models as well as technology. Changes in cost, reusability, process, and strategy mean much more can be done for much less. Therefore, adopt a scalable, cost-effective strategy encompassing business models, development models, and technology to deliver products to market faster and cheaper without sacrificing future growth.

Overview: Doing More with Less

In Web 2.0, business models need to scale as well as the technologies that implement them. By adopting a lightweight, scalable approach, many traditional costs and risks can be reduced. Less upfront capital is required before seeing a return on investment (ROI). No longer are large software development teams needed before applications go live. No longer are large marketing budgets needed to get the word out. No longer do you need to build all your e-commerce components in-house. Why? Consider:

- **Commoditization.** Commoditized hardware, bandwidth, and software have driven prices lower by an order of magnitude.

- **Reuse.** Powerful open source software, such as Linux, Apache, MySQL, and PHP (the LAMP stack), combined with large libraries of prebuilt components, have made it practical to create sophisticated web sites on short schedules and shoestring budgets.

- **Strategy:** Lessons of the dot-com bust encourage significantly leaner approaches to new business financing and product development.

- **Network effects.** Viral word-of-mouth approaches to marketing and promotion combine with revenue models that scale with adoption.

- **Process.** Adoption of agile development processes, highly iterative product cycles, and tighter customer engagement reduce cost, time, and risk.

If the model for Web 1.0 era companies was "get big fast," today it's "small is the new big."[73] Craigslist is one of the Internet's largest and most successful sites but has a staff of 22. Flickr served more than 1,000 transactions per second and 2 million photos on less than a dozen low-cost servers using free open source software on every platform layer from web servers to databases. The small site iPod Radar earns revenue from e-commerce transactions with no e-commerce infrastructure of its own. It is the Web as a platform-development philosophy extended to business models.

Benefits

- Faster time to market
- Faster ROI through reduced cost and time
- Reduced risk of project and product failure
- Greater adaptability

Best Practices

- **Scale with demand.** In an era driven by network effects, nearly every aspect of your business and product should be designed to start small and scale with demand: the technology model, the revenue model, and even the human resources model. On the demand side of the market, the essential dynamics of network effects are becoming more prominent: gradual early growth with a potential inflection point from which exponential growth kicks-in. On the supply side, new lower-cost economics allow for greater flexibility in scaling the technology, the marketing, and staff. Digg, the popular peer-driven news site, started with $2,000, a single hosted server ($99 per-month), free open source software, and an outsourced $10 per-hour developer from Elance. By fall 2006, Digg was serving more than 100 million page views a day and more than 90 servers, but had a staff size of only 15.[74]

- **Syndicate business models.** In the Internet's networked economy, there's now an online ecosystem of plug-in modular components and syndicated business models that enable enterprises to build all or part of their business on top of components from others. For example, by simply inserting a few lines of code into your web site, you can immediately begin earning advertising revenue, conducting e-commerce transactions, or performing functions from search to chat. Not long ago these components would have required substantial effort, time, and cost to build. Google AdSense epitomizes business model syndication: content publishers use AdSense by inserting a snippet of JavaScript code into their web sites and can begin displaying contextually relevant ads and earning revenue that same day. Retail e-commerce syndication was pioneered by Amazon.com through its affiliate program and now more than 1 million affiliates—web sites ranging from personal blogs to large specialized storefronts—receive commission revenue from Amazon.com each time a customer clicks-through to purchase products. Also, look for ways to integrate other business models into yours, as well as how to syndicate your own business to other businesses.

Figure 39: Incorporating various free services with HTML or JavaScript

Side Money

For a lesson of leveraging syndicated business models and outsourced services, take the popular blog of venture capitalist Fred Wilson (*http://avc.blogs.com*). He has incorporated services from more than 15 other companies into his site by only including HTML or JavaScript snippets. Often these are free services with premium upgrades (many of which Fred has upgraded to, some of which come from his portfolio of companies). These services include: e-commerce revenue (music and book links via the Amazon.com affiliate program), advertising network revenue (via the Federated Media Publishing network), syndicated advertising revenue (via Google AdSense and Yahoo! Publisher Network), the blog itself (hosted at blogs.com), blog posts via email (via the FeedBlitz service), search (via a Yahoo! widget), RSS feed services (via FeedBurner), blog link tracking (via MyBlogLog), distributed blog comment tracking (via coComment), photo "badge" of his own pictures (via Flickr), in-line ability to play music (via Streampad), music playlists (via Last.fm), business data search (via Alacra Store), job listings (via Indeed), and traffic tracking (via SiteMeter) (see Figure 39).

- **Outsource whenever practical and possible.** As certain classes of information technology become utility services, they cease being strategic advantages. We see this occurring on many levels from base infrastructure of storage and raw computing power up through software development, test, and operations management. Opportunities now exist for strategically outsourcing at each level and very rarely should one handle all of these in-house. This practice can apply equally well to two-person startups through multinationals. For example, the pay-as-you-go model of Amazon S3, which provides world-class on-demand storage with zero upfront cost, has been a cost-effective model for the small startup Altexa as well as for Microsoft. Beyond the infrastructure level, evaluate each discreet aspect of the development and operations lifecycle to determine where to outsource nonstrategic functions. Globalized outsourcing makes low-cost development, support, and operations available to companies of all sizes.

- **Provide outsourced infrastructure, function, and expertise.** This is the flipside of outsourcing whenever possible; capitalize on the new opportunities in fulfilling a new or unmet need for a growing array of outsourced infrastructures, functions, and expertise. MySpace focuses on its core competencies of social networking and outsources specialized services, such as photo management, to companies like Photobucket. In fact, 3 of the top-10 photo-sharing sites receive more traffic from MySpace than anywhere else.[75] By outsourcing its video streaming to Limelight Networks, YouTube was able to scale its business significantly faster than if it had attempted to manage these services in-house. The startup FeedBurner capitalized on an unmet need for bloggers by providing easy-to-integrate outsourced services for usage tracking, feed reliability, and integrated advertising. By July 2006, it was managing more than 19 million subscriptions for 214,000 publishers (another example of a Long Tail business model). New companies, such as ActiveGrid and 3Tera, are looking to provide virtualized web hosting with self-service provisioning designed specifically to target small to midsize Web 2.0 companies.

Marketing Virally

The decentralized user-centered nature of Web 2.0 means that user-initiated positive word-of-mouth can lead to dramatic market growth via network effects. By September 2006, more than 500,000 users visited Digg.com every day, yet the company never spent a single dollar on advertising. Some implementation ideas: make user-initiated publicity as easy as YouTube does—at the end of each video is a "Share This Video" button that makes it one-click simple to forward. Consider including links to "Email This Story" or send it to social bookmarking sites, blogs, and social news sites. Create widgets and other extremely simple to integrate plug-in components users can bring back to their own sites, blogs, and profiles (see Flickr's badges, the Yelp blogger widget, and the WeatherBug widget). Open a feedback loop with customers via company/product/staff blogs (e.g., Dell's direct2dell.com, 37signals' Signal versus Noise, or Flickr's FlickrBlog).

- **Scale your pricing and revenue models.** Now that software is increasingly provided as an online service and no longer purchased as a shrink-wrapped application, some traditional software sales and pricing models no longer apply. In their place are a set of more flexible and scalable models. And the most successful online pricing and revenue strategies are not a one-size-fits-all approach but instead incorporate multiple revenue streams and scalable, tiered pricing models. Thus pricing and revenue align with the core attributes and patterns of Web 2.0 (see Table 4):

    — Network effects are encouraged through low-cost, low-barrier adoption and provide an upgrade path

    — Free or low-cost pricing leverages the Long Tail by encouraging widespread adoption, even for individuals and small operations

    — Advertising models support a platform strategy via SaaS that is free or lower in cost to the user

    — Maintaining reasonable user costs encourages participation, which in turns helps foster growth, community, and, ultimately, user-generated data as part of an "Intel Inside" data strategy

Table 4: Web 2.0 revenue model

Revenue model	Pros	Cons	Examples
Syndicated advertising	• Users get free content and services • Free or low price encourages adoption	• Not always targeted effectively • Not appropriate for all scenarios (e.g., behind enterprise firewall)	• Google AdSense text-based contextual ads • Ad network models such as Federated Media Publishing or AdBrite
Sponsorship advertising	• Users get free content and services • Free or low price encourages adoption • Ads may be better matched to content and audience	• Not as widely scalable from a Long Tail perspective	• Advertising variant with direct relationship between advertiser and publisher • TechCrunch
Subscriptions	• Simplicity • Recurring revenue model • Low or no-cost startup for users encourages adoption (can be step-up from ad supported free version) • Flat rate or variable (by usage) options	• Cost deters some users • Some customers prefer more traditional licensing models (e.g., IT departments)	• Salesforce.com's services • 37signals' Basecamp • (Note that many of the premium services are offered as pay-as-you-go subscription services)
Transaction commissions	• Tied directly to customer actions • Allows partners to share revenue	• Not suitable for all business models	• Amazon.com and eBay affiliate programs
Premium services	• Attractive upgrade option for free and ad-supported customers	• Some customers will not opt for upgrades	• Flickr Pro and Flickr photo printing • FeedBurner Total Stats service • Microsoft Office Live
Product licensing	• Most traditional and familiar model	• Less flexibility and scalability • Not well suited to SaaS	• Traditional desktop software such as Microsoft Office • Traditional enterprise software such as SAP and Oracle

- **Fail fast, scale fast.** Succeeding in Web 2.0 requires innovation, but innovation requires risk. To mitigate these risks, adopt a fail fast, scale fast philosophy that encourages new ideas and experimentation but recognizes that failure happens—the sooner you can change and move on, the better. Speed is crucial, both in execution and decision-making.

- **Design for scale.** Scalability does not happen by accident. Start early with strategic and tactical choices that will enable scaling as the business or product grows.

    - **Simplicity scales.** Rapid growth is fostered by avoiding complex solutions, particularly in technology choices and designs.

    - **Self-service scales.** As many Long Tail businesses prove, empowering users with self-service tools gives them more control and simultaneously keeps operating and support costs down. The impact of this is amplified at scale.

    - **Emergent systems scale.** Google search results emerge as users create content and links. Both eBay and Craigslist facilitate emergence. Wikipedia scaled to more than 1 million entries (more than 10 times the size of *Encyclopedia Britannica*) by virtue of its open, decentralized, and emergent design.

Issues & Debates

- **Sunk by network effects.** Exponential growth is wonderful as long as it doesn't catch you flatfooted—it has sabotaged more than one Web 2.0 product. Rapid, network-driven growth helped derail the Friendster service with near fatal performance and service reliability issues.[76] Even MySpace, while in the process of overtaking Friendster, underwent substantial changes to manage its rapid growth. In less than 3 years of operation, it grew to 3 data centers, 2,682 web servers, 90 cache servers, 60 database servers, 150 media-processing servers, 1,000 SAN storage disks, and it consumes 17,000 MB per second of bandwidth.[77]

- **If you can build it cheap and fast, so can the next guy.** Low barriers to entry are a classic double-edged sword. This is evident by the current glut of Web 2.0 startups, many begun on tiny budgets or even as personal side projects. As in earlier eras of rapid growth and innovation, few of these will survive, but those with a legitimate business model and a true understanding of Web 2.0 best practices have the strongest chance.

- **Advertising dependencies.** Not every online business can rely on advertising as its sole or primary revenue source. The ad market goes through cycles, and by creating a diversified revenue model, including subscription and premium services, companies can build long-term growth and stability.

Misconceptions

- **Having no revenue model is a viable approach**. Although growth and user acquisition matter, they are not the end game. Business sustainability ultimately requires real revenue.

Enterprise 2.0 Recommendations

- **Build lightweight scaling into enterprise architecture.** Too often a one-size-fits-all enterprise architecture increases complexity and development costs by failing to appropriately scale solutions to needs. Define an architecture strategy that allows IT systems to start from a stance of scalable simplicity and add complexity as required.

- **Change what "enterprise class" means.** For decades, the phrase "enterprise class" symbolized large-scale software, anything from global ERP systems to giant data warehouses. From purely a global-scaling perspective, today's consumer-facing Web 2.0 applications may force a change in definition where a single service, such as MySpace, adds more new accounts in a few days than the global workforce size of HP, Microsoft, Dell, IBM, and Sun combined. The demands on these massive, interactive, data-intensive systems exceeds most of what the corporate world has seen, and IT departments may now be getting lessons in scaling from the outside.

Related Patterns

- **Perpetual Beta.** Agile, lightweight development processes and tools complement lightweight business models.

- **Innovation in Assembly.** Platforms facilitate scaling and encourage others to do work and innovate for you.

SECTION III
Web 2.0 Exemplars

If there are eight core patterns that define Web 2.0, then what are the companies that are most successfully applying those principles? This section examines two perspectives:

- **Exemplars matrix.** Ten Web 2.0 leaders are reviewed in the context of these patterns. This model shows the relationship of Web 2.0 patterns as used across the industry, as well as highlights the strengths and weaknesses (or gaps) in the application of Web 2.0 practices. Companies are listed left to right by start date, which shows a mix of early pioneers that capitalized on the Web's unique traits, as well as newer startups that built on these lessons (see Table 5).

- **Case studies.** Two of these exemplars successfully used, or in some cases defined, Web 2.0 best practices. Two very different types of online businesses are examined from two very different generations: Amazon.com demonstrates how a company born in the Web's first era successfully evolved into a Web 2.0 company, while the much newer Flickr was born with many of the genetics of Web 2.0 at its core. The former has a more traditional transactional business model whereas the latter focuses on consumer-generated digital content.

Table 5: Web 2.0 Exemplars Matrix

		Amazon	eBay	Craigslist	Google
Background	Founded	1995	1995	1995	1998
	Web site	amazon.com	ebay.com	craigslist.org	google.com
	Alexa ranking (as of October 2006)	14	12	29	3
Pattern	Harnessing Collective Intelligence	• User reviews • Recommendations • Product wikis	• Reputation system • Blogs and wikis	• Classifieds marketplace	• PageRank • Google AdSense
	Data Is the Next "Intel Inside"	• Product catalog and sales history • User reviews and other content	• Auction data • Buyer/seller data	• Classifieds data	• Search index • AdWords data • Google Base
	Innovation in Assembly	• APIs • RSS • Amazon Services	• APIs • RSS	• RSS	• APIs • Operations reliability • Gadgets • RSS
	Rich User Experiences	• Most pages dynamic per user			• Maps • GMail • Google Suggest
	Perpetual Beta	• Metrics and sampling	• Releases every two weeks	• Incremental releases	• Public betas of most products • Google Labs
	Software Above the Level of a Single Device	• Amazon Anywhere	• eBay Wireless		• m.google.com
	Leveraging the Long Tail	• Back catalog • Affiliates program • Collaborative filtering • Self-service	• Self-service	• Self-service	• AdSense • AdWords • Google Base • Self-service
	Lightweight Business and Cost-Effective Scalability			• Started as side project • Staff of 22	• More than 450,000 commodity servers[78]

58   Web 2.0 Principles and Best Practices

Wikipedia	del.icio.us	MySpace	Eventful	Flickr	YouTube
2001	2003	2003	2004	2004	2005
wikipedia.org	del.icio.us	myspace.com	eventful.com	flickr.com	youtube.com
17	156	6	32,369	39	10
• All content is user contributed	• User and group value • Popularity rankings	• Social network • Groups	• User calendars • Sharing, grouping • Groups	• Photos • Tags • Groups • Collaborative filters	• Viral marketing • Groups
• Reference data • GFDL	• Bookmarks and metadata • User RSS via Creative Commons	• User content • Group data	• Event database • Venue and performers database	• User photos and metadata • Creative Commons models	• Video data • Metadata
• API planned	• API • RSS	• Third-party tools and widgets	• API • iCalendar • RSS • Alerts	• API • RSS of photos, tags, and groups	• API • Pluggable widgets • RSS
	• Ajax forms • Organizr	• Rich media support	• Ajax	• Ajax	• Ajax • Flash-based rich media playback
• Incremental releases	• Incremental releases	• Incremental releases	• Incremental releases • Eventful labs	• Releases daily or weekly	• Incremental releases
		• MySpace Mobile		• Flickr Mobile	• Mobile video uploads
• Decentralized contribution model	• Self-service • Collaborative filtering	• Self-service	• Collaborative filtering • Eventful Demand service	• Uses AdSense • Fed blogging ecosystem • Self-service • Collaborative filtering	• Uses AdSense • Fed social network ecosystem • Self-service • Collaborative filtering
• One server in 2002 • Less than five employees	• Initially a one man corporation • Started as side project			• Small funding • Multiple revenue streams	• Multiple revenue streams

WEB 2.0 PROFILE

Amazon.com

Leading the Way from Web 1.0 to Web 2.0

Amazon.com, founded by entrepreneur Jeff Bezos in 1995, pioneered online retailing. Reaching prominence as "The Earth's Biggest Bookstore" during the initial dot-com boom, Amazon.com has not only survived but thrived. It has 59 million active customer accounts and serves as an exemplar of many of the techniques now recognized as central to a successful Web 2.0 strategy.

This case study examines how Amazon.com transitioned from a Web 1.0 to a Web 2.0 company—hoping to define Web 2.0 in the process—by leveraging the best practices described in this report (see Figure 40).

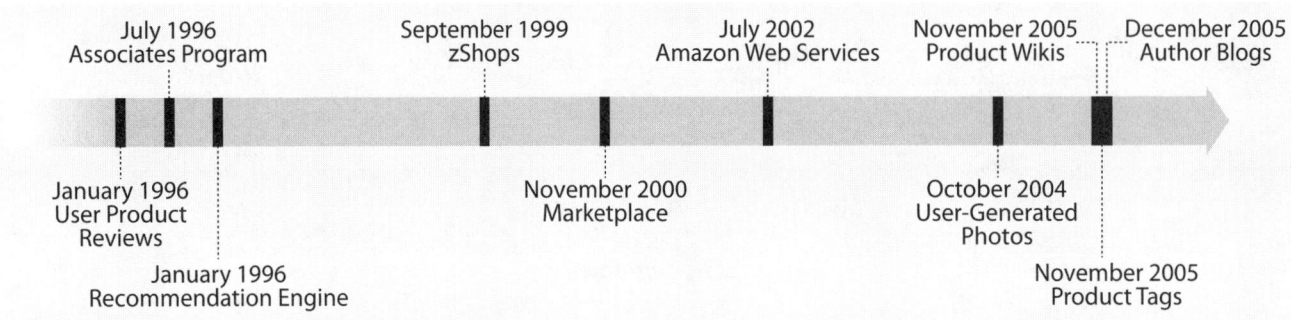

Figure 40: *Amazon.com Web 2.0 timeline*

Amazon.com Profile by Web 2.0 Pattern

❶ Harnessing Collective Intelligence

Amazon.com accomplishes paying the user first with a best-in-class retail shopping experience. In 2005, the Annual Customer Satisfaction Index (ACSI) for Amazon.com was 87 out of a possible 100, the highest score of any retail and online service company.[79]

Figure 41: *Amazon.com's rate this item icon*

Building from that core shopping experience, Amazon.com has repeatedly demonstrated how an architecture of participation can be created on top of what is otherwise a commodity business. Beginning with essentially the same data and products as early competitors, such as Barnes & Noble, Amazon.com aggressively built features that invited customer involvement and contribution. One of Amazon.com's most enduring successes is customer product reviews. Rather than relying solely on the traditional models of professional reviewers and in-house editorial, Amazon.com created a simple mechanism for any visitor to submit her own reviews, good or bad, and have those comments appear right alongside of the product itself (see Figure 41). By doing so, Amazon.com began harnessing collective intelligence. While others have used customer product reviews, no company has persued user enhancement of its product catalog as aggressively and as intelligently as Amazon.com.

Since that time, Amazon.com has progressively added ways for involving customers both implicitly and explicitly, so many so that the best means to understand them is to dissect a typical product page from their site. Figure 42 shows more than a dozen unique Web 2.0 elements within a single product page; nearly half of the content in a typical product page is user-generated. Within the page the user is regularly invited to participate and contribute content, for example, "Write an online review," "Tag this product," "Rate this item," "Create your guide," "Share your own customer images," and "Was this review helpful to you?" (see Table 6).

Table 6: Amazon.com product page elements

Customer product reviews	Product reviews written by Amazon.com customers.
Listmania	Customer-created lists on any subject with links to relevant products in the catalog.
Customer product images	Amazon.com likens these to "visual reviews" that help other customers see how products are used.
Submit a product manual	Customers may upload product manuals.
User guides	Customer with knowledge or expertise on a particular topic can create guides for other customers.
Email to a friend	Customers can forward product links to other potential customers.
Product tags	Classify products by assigning tags (keywords).
Product wiki	Customers can collaboratively edit a wiki for each product to enhance the core product description.
Product discussion forum	A product-specific discussion forum integrated within the page; customers can initiate and join threads.
Rate this	Products can be rated (voted) using a 1 to 5 star system. Aggregate totals and averages are used within the product summary.
Recommendation engine	Product recommendations are based on collective user purchasing behavior.
Amazon connect	Author blogs are hosted on Amazon.com.
What do customers ultimately buy after viewing items like this?	Listing of four other items purchased by customers who have previously viewed an item.
Customers who bought this also bought	Listing of four items purchased by customers who previously purchased this item.
Reviewing rating	Provides feedback on quality of other customers' reviews.
Report this	Customers can report inappropriate content written by other customers.
Comment on reviews	Customers can directly comment on reviews from other customers.
Profile pages	Self-profiles aggregate reviews, images, lists, and other information posted by that customer. Allows customers to decide what information to share (via levels of trust, such as Me, Friends, and Everyone) and to establish friend lists.
Sell yours	Convenient entry point to Amazon Marketplace allowing customers to sell the same item.

Figure 42: Web 2.0 elements of an Amazon.com product page

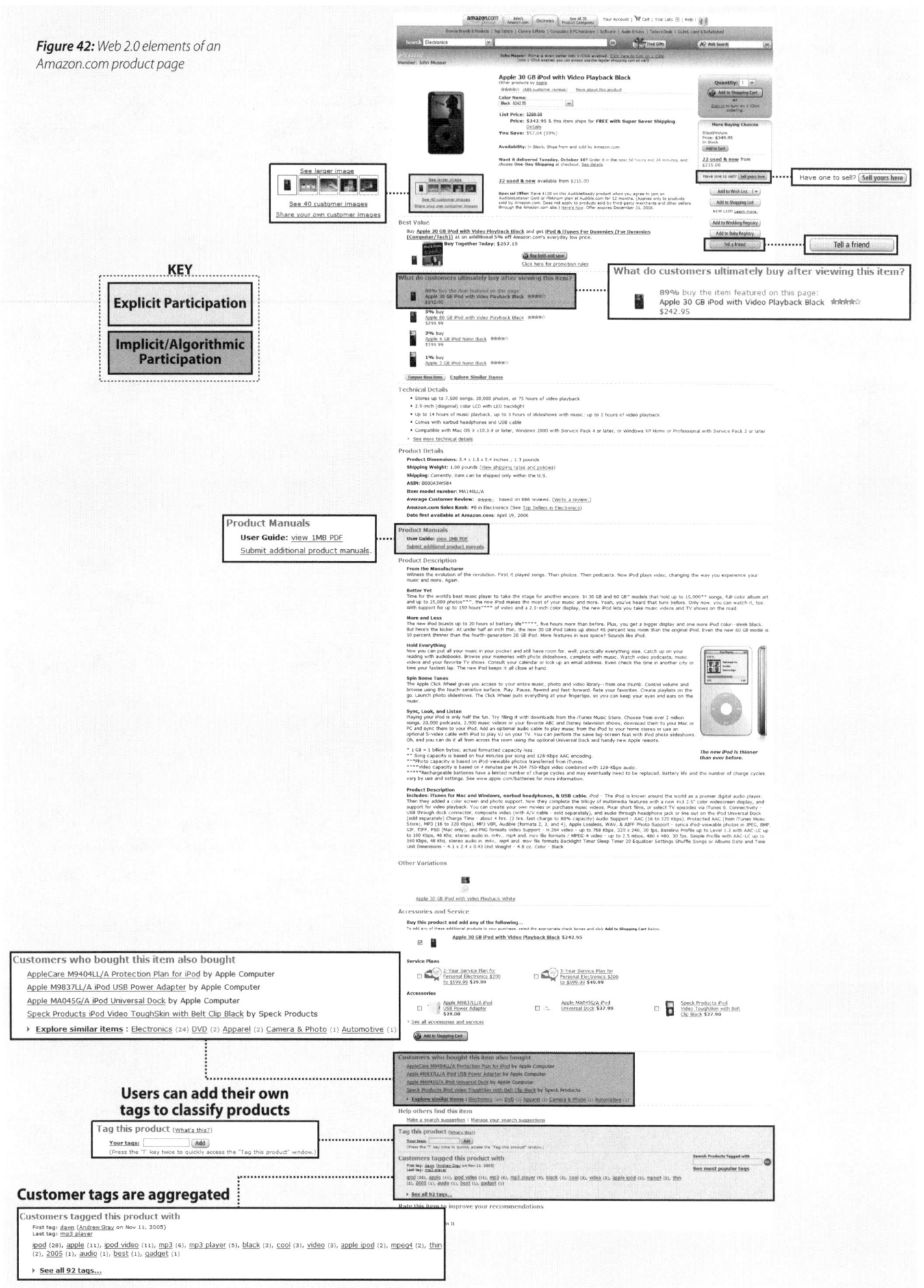

Figure 42 (continued): Web 2.0 elements of an Amazon.com product page

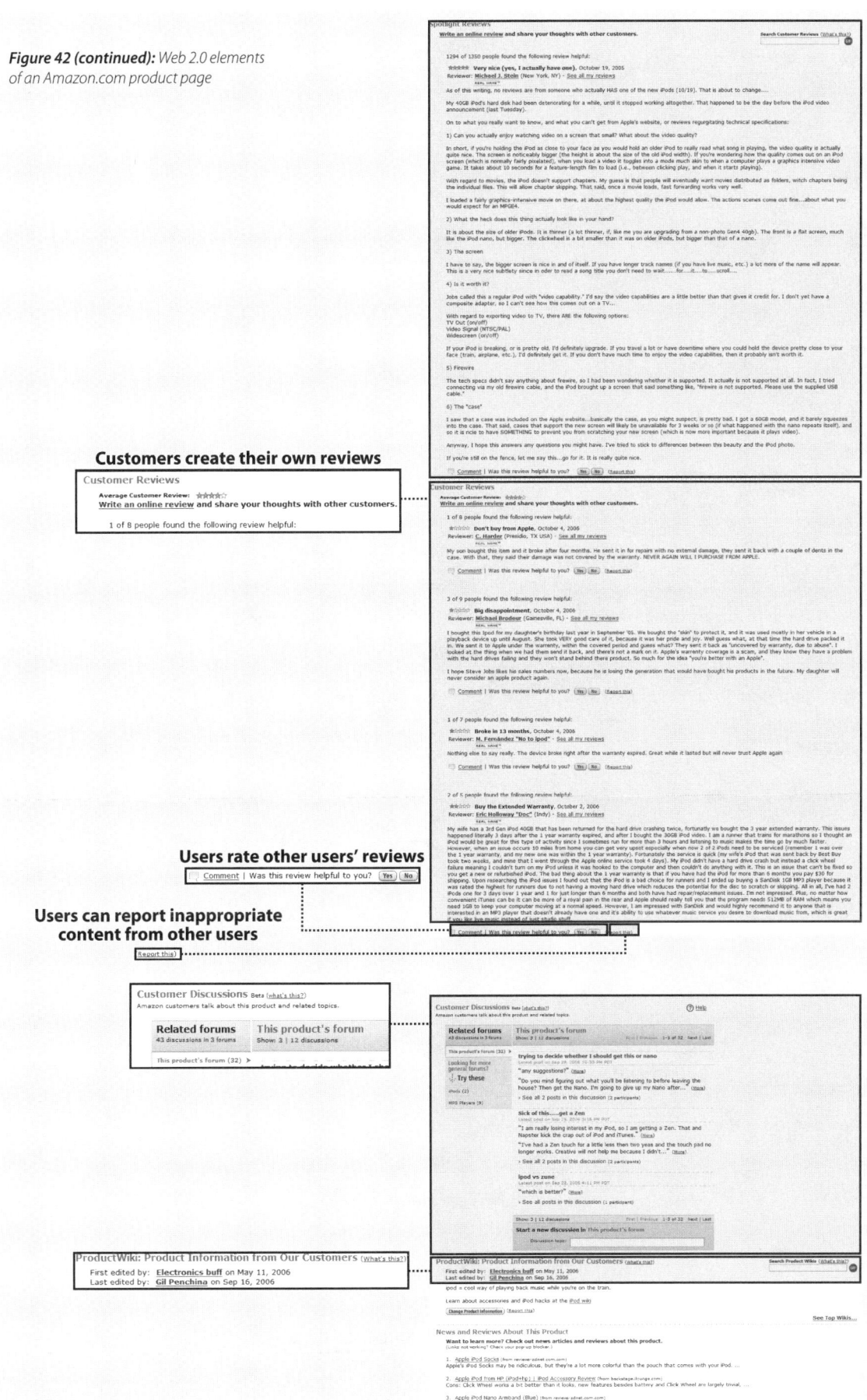

Section III: Web 2.0 Exemplars

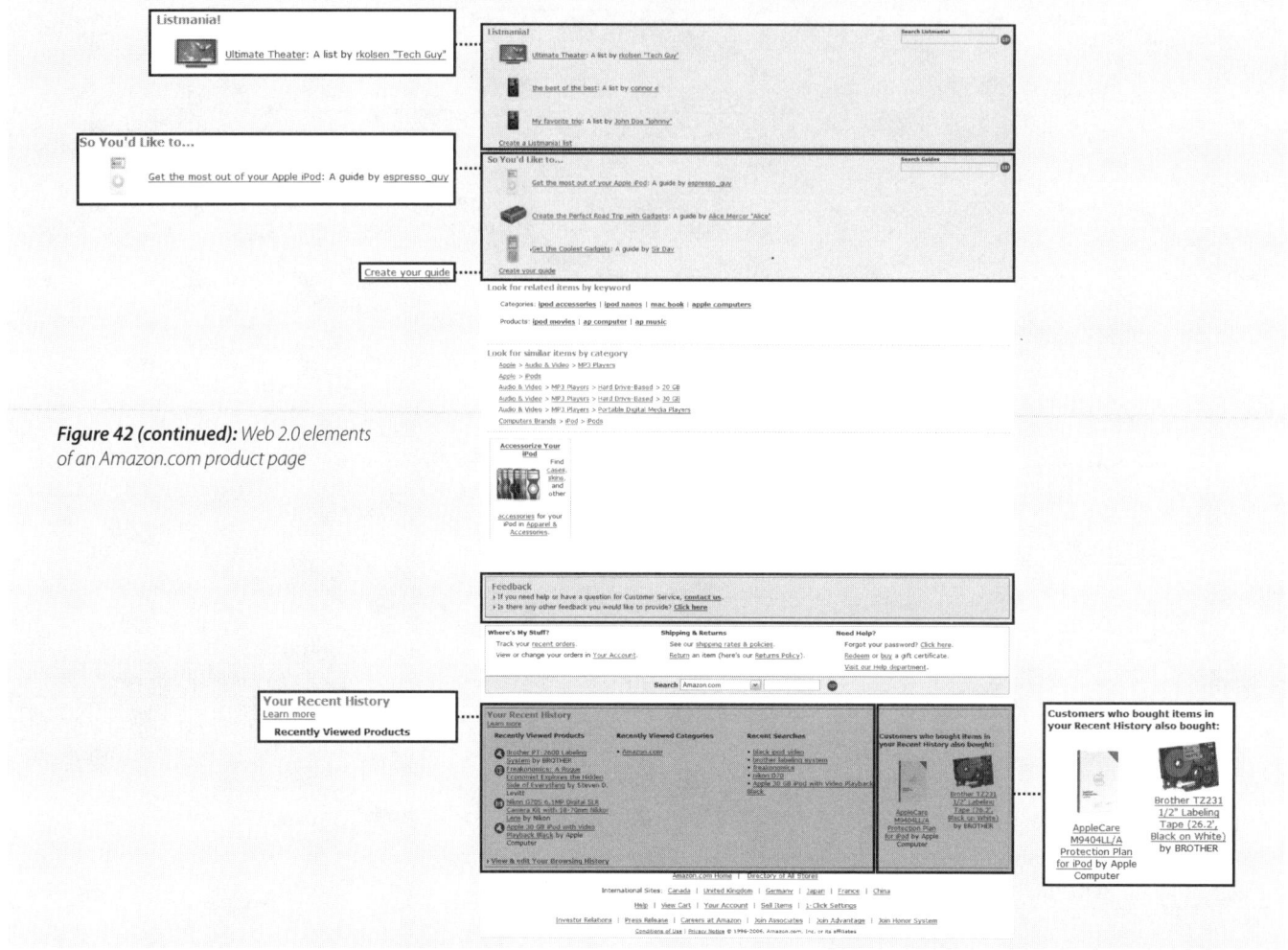

Figure 42 (continued): Web 2.0 elements of an Amazon.com product page

If you compare this product page against the same product profile at Barnes & Noble, you'll see a much more limited architecture of participation—only four elements,[80] less than one-third as many forms of customer engagement. Although more does not always mean better, the extent of Amazon.com's customer loyalty and its valuable customer-generated content demonstrates the strategic value of these practices. Competitors such as Barnes & Noble also violate the "pay the user first" principle by intermixing sponsored results or promotions with search results. Amazon.com's default search result, "most popular," is based on dozens of functions. All focused on discovery and responding to what the user really wants.

Controlling the Wisdom of Crowds at Amazon.com

Amazon.com has instituted a variety of policies and controls. Its guideline for users uploading product images is "Behave as if you were a guest at a friend's dinner party: please treat the Amazon.com community with respect." Photos with objectionable content, personally identifiable information, or unrelated images are prohibited. Customers must also create a "Real Name" signature that matches the name on their credit card. Product reviews are moderated according to set of guidelines[81] and reviews deemed inappropriate are removed by Amazon.com staff.

A critical success factor for Amazon.com was trusting its users. The notion that negative customer reviews would be permitted alongside products a retailer was actively promoting ran contrary to all prior commerce models. And although at times negative customer reviews may have reduced sales for specific products, the overall impact created customer loyalty and trust.

Amazon.com is designed to improve the more people use it, which happens at multiple levels starting with the one of the world's premier recommendation engines. The relevance of suggestions from Amazon.com's engine increases as more customers act and transact within the system. Click-through and conversion rates measurably improve via automated collaborative filtering mechanisms, including an item-to-item model of similarity metrics of products that customers tend to purchase together.[82]

In aggregate, the value of directly contributed customer data increases: two customer reviews might be an unreliable sample, but on a larger scale, while still a self-selecting population, they become more meaningful. Amazon.com has more than 10 million customers reviews. As of spring 2006, *The DaVinci Code* had more than 3,400 customer reviews (see Figure 43). The catalog entry for an Apple iPod had 39 customer-contributed images, a forum with 8 ongoing discussions, and a variety of related user-created lists and guides.

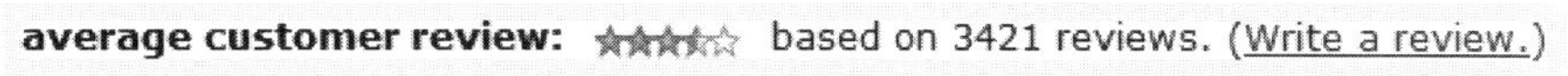

Figure 43: *Amazon.com's average customer review display*

In 2006, Amazon.com introduced a feature that builds even further on customer reviews. It gave customers a structured way to directly comment on the reviews of other readers. In essence, these may make reviews more like conversations and, in turn, lead to an even greater degree of user participation.

Because collaborative filtering techniques are not foolproof and can be skewed by certain types of data—e.g., a consumer purchases a gift but that item should not be added to his recommendation profile—Amazon.com provides a mechanism, via "Improve Your Recommendations" to allow direct user input into the algorithm. This can improve recommendation and search relevancy, which leads to higher sales.

❷ Data Is the Next "Intel Inside"

Since its founding 1995 Amazon.com has amassed vast warehouses of data, and although much of it is based on customer transaction history, even more of it is directly contributed by customers. No other online retailer has the depth or breadth of valuable publisher-supplied and user-contributed content. Amazon.com successfully employed an architecture of participation to not only grow its business but, together with customers, it enhanced the core data and ultimately produced a hard-to-recreate user-generated database that has become its "Intel Inside" advantage.

Amazon.com's data-driven strategic advantage is further enhanced by the ASIN—its proprietary product identification system. Individuals, organizations, and even researchers use ASIN identifiers because they are unique identifiers that build on industry standards (for books, the ASIN is the same as the book's ISBN), user enrichment of the base data has created a richer data set, and Amazon.com's affiliate program often creates an economic incentive for linking to Amazon.com. In effect, Amazon.com adopted an embrace and extend strategy for data; subsequently, the ASIN has become a way to control the namespace for this data.

❸ Innovation in Assembly

Amazon.com was one of the first online properties to leverage its technology infrastructure and turn its web site into a web platform. Amazon Services (*http://amazon-services.com*) is a subsidiary of Amazon.com, specifically focused on providing these technologies and services. One of Amazon Services' core offerings is providing fully outsourced, private label web sites for other retailers, including Target, Toys "R" Us, and NBA.com.

Amazon Services also offers a suite of web service APIs. Begun in 2002, there are now 10 sets of APIs and approximately 180,000 developers registered in the Amazon Web Services (AWS) program. The AWS program is the latest strategic element of a broader partner and technology platform strategy that includes the Amazon Associate's Program, zShops, and Amazon Marketplace.

There are three basic pricing models used across the various APIs, all of which offer a commercial use license:

- Free with shared revenue model; e.g., E-Commerce Service
- Fixed monthly fee; e.g., Amazon Historical Pricing
- Usage/resource-based; e.g., Amazon S3 and Elastic Compute Cloud (Amazon EC2)

By making the E-Commerce Web Service an extension of its profitable affiliate program, every web service transaction that results in a product sale generates revenue for Amazon.com. External developers design, build, and promote their own applications, Amazon.com provides the platform, and both parties share in the proceeds. Developers are effectively creating web services-based franchises for Amazon.com. As a by-product of this arrangement, one built on shared interests, Amazon.com is also building loyalty and reinforcing viral network effects.

Amazon.com's APIs

The APIs fall into four general families: e-commerce, infrastructure, web, and workflow. The usage and resource based services, such as S3, are built on a metered, pay-as-you-go model that can scale for both the provider and customer. This is a new, evolving model of utility computing where shared resources are provisioned and paid for based on resources used rather than a flat-rate (akin to the electrical power industry). This can be a very cost-effective model for a variety of scenarios and businesses. For example, online photo-sharing service SmugMug estimates it has saved approximately $500,000 in storage costs by using Amazon S3.[83]

Amazon.com CEO Jeff Bezos points out that, "The dirty little secret is that at least 70 percent of the time, energy, and dollars [of web entrepreneurs] go into this back-end heavy-lifting infrastructure. You can transition from something that was a large fixed cost—from the lone developer to the venture-backed company—to be a variable cost." Amazon.com has invested $2 billion on infrastructure since its founding, so providing these services via APIs is a small incremental cost. "The reason we're doing this is because we think we can empower developers with a new kind of web-scale technology. And we can make a profitable business for ourselves."[84] said Bezos.

Amazon.com is building a multiformat data strategy: RSS in now part of its syndicated content, delivering feeds of product categories and searches. It followed API best practices by supporting multiple protocols including SOAP and REST. It was also managed via developer keys and self-service setup, as well as full documentation and developer support. Examples were provided for the most popular programming languages. Amazon.com uses both traditional developer support—discussion forums, email newsletters, and FAQ—as well as Web 2.0 techniques to support its platform, including RSS feeds of platform news and an Amazon Web Services blog.

To balance the needs of the company and developers, Amazon.com's API licensing imposes certain constraints on how the APIs can be used. For example, Amazon E-Commerce Service allows no more than 1 API call per second, pricing data may be stored for a maximum of 1 hour and non-price data for a maximum of 24 hours, data may not be re-sold, and a link back to Amazon.com is required. These requirements are not generally considered unreasonable and are consistent with the limits of other providers (see Table 7 and Figure 44).

Table 7: Amazon.com's web service offerings

API	Description	Pricing/Revenue model
E-Commerce Service	Search and retrieve detailed product catalog data, has some shopping cart capabilities.	No cost service for members of the Amazon Affiliate Program. Revenue is shared for transactions, the same as affiliate terms (typically 4 to 8.5 percent).
Mechanical Turk	Marketplace for matching micro-level work tasks with service providers. A massively scalable peer-production framework.85	No upfront fee, Amazon.com charges a 10 percent commission to requesters.
S3	Online storage service designed for cost-effective, scalable, low-latency storage with high reliability.	No upfront fee, $0.10 per 1,000 messages sent and $0.20 per GB of data transferred.
EC2	Pay as you go hosted computing. Dynamically resizable capacity.	$0.10 per instance-hour consumed, $0.20 per GB of data transferred outside of Amazon.com, $0.15 per GB-month of Amazon S3 storage.
Simple Queue Service	Hosted service for queuing messages between distributed application components.	No upfront fee, $0.10 per 1,000 messages sent and $0.20 per GB of data transferred.
Amazon Historical Pricing	Access to three years of sales data for books, music, and videos.	Subscription fee is $499 for up to 20,000 requests per month, or $999 for up to 60,000 requests per month.
Alexa Top Sites	Web site traffic ranking data.	$0.0025 per URL returned.
Alexa Web Information Service	Programmatic access to web traffic data, web search, web link maps, and web crawl metadata.	First 10,000 requests per month are free, additional requests are $0.00015 per request.
Alexa Site Thumbnail	Programmatic access to thumbnail images of web site home pages.	$0.0002 per thumbnail returned.
Alexa Web Search	Web search through 4 billion documents and 300 TBs of Alexa indexed data.	First 10,000 requests per month are free, additional requests are $0.00015 per request.

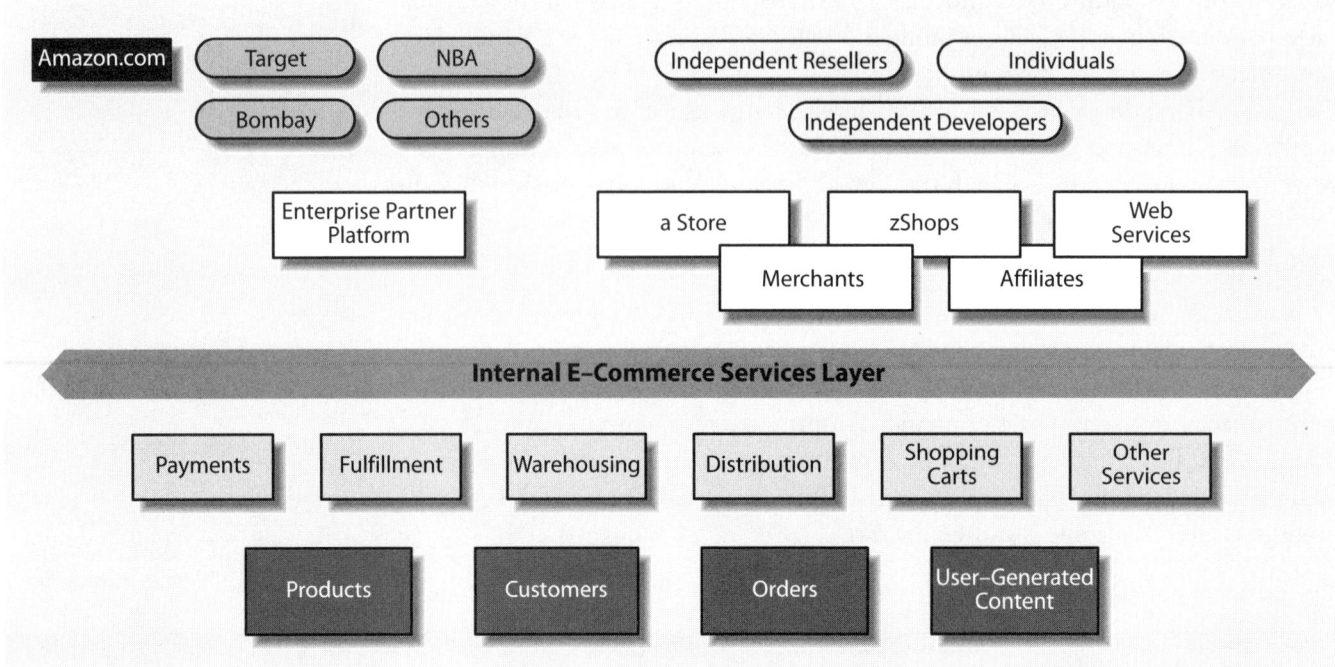

Figure 44: Distribution of Amazon.com's e-commerce services

Examples of Third-Party Applications Using Amazon.com APIs

Monsoon offers marketplace management services to help offline companies sell merchandise online. Monsoon uses the Amazon E-Commerce API as part of its offerings. The result: 20 percent of Amazon.com's top 50 marketplace sellers manage their sales with Monsoon (see Figure 45).

Figure 45: Monsoon using Amazon's E-Commerce API

CastingWords is a podcast transcription service. Customers submit digital audio podcasts and pay a per-minute fee to have the content converted to text. The CastingWords service then uses Amazon's Mechanical Turk service to match the podcasts with external transcribers who perform the actual transcription (see Figure 46).

Figure 46: CastingWords using Amazon's Mechanical Turk API

SmugMug is a photo-sharing service with 15 employees and 150,000 paying customers. It has almost half a billion images stored and will save approximately $500,000 in 2006 by using S3. Development to operation took one week (see Figure 47).

Figure 47: SmugMug using Amazon's S3 API

❹ Rich User Experiences

Relative to the size and scope of the Amazon.com service, changes to the user experience are modest and do not, as of the third quarter of 2006, represent a dramatic change from earlier generations of web interfaces. This is in visible contrast to Web 2.0-born applications such as Flickr.

Recently there has been some incremental addition of rich media and Ajax features including dynamic menus, in-place navigation, and dynamic feedback (see Figure 48).

Much of the value in the Amazon.com user experience derives from extensive content personalization: nearly every page presented to a given user at Amazon.com is created on-the-fly for that specific user, including the Amazon.com home page itself.

❺ The Perpetual Beta

Not only is Development 2.0 alive and well at Amazon.com, much of it has been battle-tested during the past decade on its site with real-time sampling and testing, agile development models, and closing the gap between building software and running software.

Figure 48: Ajax features incorporated into Amazon.com

Every time a customer visits Amazon.com she may be acting as a real-time tester and co-developer of new product features and services. Amazon.com runs A/B-style tests of new features on its production site every day, incrementally adding new features and products. As a matter of fact, so many tests are run that one of its key challenges is making sure multiple experiments don't conflict by touching the same feature.[86] Nearly all features that ultimately go live on Amazon.com's site are tested, including page designs, algorithms for recommendations, feature placement, and search relevance rankings. Amazon.com measures according to the nature of the change, but also included are transactional measures, including units and revenue, behavioral measures, such as session time, and the number of steps it takes to complete a specific transaction.

Key lessons from Amazon.com's experience include:

- Data trumps intuition (i.e., use product instrumentation to collect specific, measurable user behavior)

- Often a prototype is easier to build than a behavioral-prediction model (i.e., real users are the most reliable test)

- Automation trumps intuition (i.e., software learns and makes decisions on the fly, such as which features or content is more effective)

Amazon.com considers the ideal development team size to be one that can feed all of its members with two pizzas. "If a project team can eat more than two pizzas, it's too large." said Werner Vogels, Amazon.com CTO.[87] Small teams employing agile methods characterize this company philosophy focused on innovation and a decentralized development model.

"You build it, you run it" is core to Amazon.com's development philosophy—developers don't just write the code, they support it on the production servers. Giving operational responsibilities to developers helps make operations a core competency at Amazon.com. This is in stark contrast to traditional software development organizations where code is often "thrown over the wall" from development to operations. By moving developers closer to both operations and to customers, Amazon.com has created a feedback loop that improves both the quality of the technology and the quality of the service.

Additionally, although programming language choice is not dictated at Amazon.com, incentives are provided for adopting tools and components that specifically improve overall service quality, such as monitoring, and other infrastructure tools.

❻ Software Above the Level of a Single Device

In 1999, Amazon.com began moving beyond the desktop by introducing Amazon Anywhere, which is the basis of its overall mobile device strategy. Individual features such as Mobile Alerts allow users of Amazon.com's auction services to be notified when they win or are outbid.

To accommodate the ever-changing myriad device form factors, Amazon.com has designed its internal web services interfaces to be independent of the device display. By then applying technologies such as external stylesheets, the content can be dynamically tailored to each application and device. Its web-based experience is modified to suit the device, e.g., by limiting search results to the top three to five matches. And Amazon.com makes simplicity a priority in its mobile device interface by prominently displaying the Amazon 1-Click feature as one of only two buttons that appear with every search result.

Overall, Amazon.com's Web 2.0 "above a single device" strategy is adequate but uninspired. With the growing movement toward both social shopping and mobile commerce there is room for improvement.

❼ Leveraging the Long Tail

Amazon.com pioneered leveraging the Long Tail a decade ago when it launched the Amazon Associates Program in 1996, which was one the very first online affiliate programs. By offering referral fees of up to 8.5 percent, this program has grown to more than 1 million members.

Other elements of the Amazon.com Long Tail strategy include:

- **zShops:** independent merchants and retailers selling products on Amazon.com
- **Marketplace:** individuals sell new, used, refurbished, and collectible items
- **CustomFlix and BookSurge:** video and print self-publishing services

Algorithmic data management begins with Amazon.com's collaborative filtering but goes much further—for example, search results. If you compare Amazon.com's results against competitors like Barnes & Noble, you often see better results at Amazon.com. As with Google's PageRank algorithm, by going beyond straight textual analysis and instead factoring in collective intelligence elements like customer reviews and customer behavior, Amazon.com is able to increase sales through better matching results to user interests. What is the most relevant for a given user does not have to equal best selling (see Figure 49).

Amazon.com has successfully leveraged customer self-service to simultaneously reduce costs and increase customer satisfaction (as noted earlier, it repeatedly scores at the top of customer satisfaction surveys for online retailers). Customers are put in control through a set of self-service tools including the My Account page, order tracking with arrival estimates, returns, and lifetime order history.

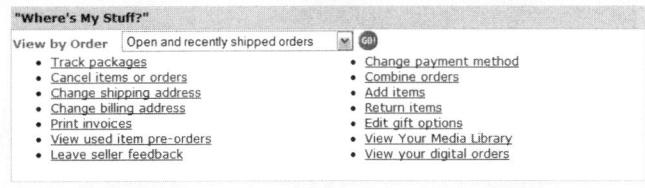

Figure 49: Self-service tools

Other elements of the Long Tail strategy include:

- Amazon aStore, introduced in August 2006, is a service that gives affiliates a simple roll-your-own storefront capability (see Figure 50). Affiliates can pick products, choose from interface templates and color schemes, and select widgets. As with other affiliate programs, revenue is via a cost per action (CPA) model, giving affiliates revenue for each completed user transaction.

- Amazon Pages offers customers the ability to purchase individual chapters of books.

- Amazon Honor System allows any web site to collect voluntary payments from its users and accept payment for digital content.[88] Amounts can be as little as $1. Amazon.com charges collecting sites 2.9 percent of the total amount and $0.30 per transaction.

Figure 50: Amazon aStore

Lightweight Business Models and Cost-Effective Scalability

As a Fortune 500 company and one born in the dot-com age of "get big fast," Amazon.com doesn't fit the mold of a lightweight organization. But it pioneers lightweight business models for others by virtue of its affiliate programs and platform strategy.

Amazon.com supports business models built on syndication. This includes individual bloggers who generate revenue by adding only a few links to the Amazon.com catalog, as well as small and large retailers that have benefited from either increased revenue or substantial infrastructure cost savings by building on the Amazon.com platform.

Many elements of Amazon.com's Long Tail strategy, such as the aStore, zShops, and Marketplace, can also be seen as facilitating lightweight business models.

Web 2.0 vs. Web 1.0: Amazon.com vs. Barnes & Noble

Amazon.com used its understanding of Web 2.0 best practices (long before the term was coined) to best competitor Barnes & Noble in the online bookseller race. Amazon.com has consistently offered many more user-participation elements on an average product page. Over the years, this has resulted in a much richer store of user-generated content. In recent years it has continued to innovate services such as APIs, syndication, product wikis, author blogs, and product tags. Even today, Barnes & Noble offers few of these features.

WEB 2.0 PROFILE
Flickr.com

Flickr is a web site for digital photo storage, sharing, and organization. Compared to earlier generations of photo sites, such as Shutterfly and Ofoto, which focused on photo-finishing services like making prints, Flickr instead provides a photo-sharing context and community.

Ludicorp, a Vancouver-based company founded in 2002, launched the Flickr service in early 2004, and was acquired by Yahoo! in March 2005. As of February 2006, more than 2 million registered users had uploaded at least 100 million photos. During its first 18 months of service, Flickr capitalized on—and in many cases defined—the best practices of this era, and symbolizing a new generation of companies born with Web 2.0 in their genes.

Flickr's business model builds on multiple revenue streams:

- Subscription-based premium accounts
- Advertising
- Complementary photo services: photo finishing, DVD creation, calendars, etc.

Flickr capitalized on a powerful combination of business, social and technological drivers: high-speed broadband, the rise of digital cameras and camera phones, low-cost infrastructure (especially storage and bandwidth), blogs and social networking, and syndication via RSS.

Flickr.com Profile by Web 2.0 Pattern

❶ Harnessing Collective Intelligence

Flickr's fundamental function is giving individuals a simple, low-cost way to store and retrieve photos online. In so doing, it pays customers first by giving immediate value with minimal barriers to adoption. All the benefits of community and network effects flow naturally downstream from this central action.

The heart and soul of Flickr is a photo-sharing community. When users upload photos to Flickr, they most often are sharing them not only with friends and family, but with communities of Flickr users and the whole Internet as well. Flickr's default photo visibility setting is public, so the network effects are set by default, this allowed Flickr to grow more than 5 to 10 percent per week during its first 18 months. After Flickr's first year, 82 percent of all photos were public (see Figure 51).[89]

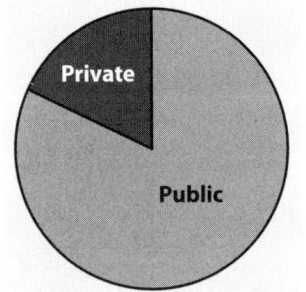

Figure 51: *Public photos on Flickr*

Flickr's architecture of participation ensures that it involves users both explicitly and implicitly. Users are actively engaged by annotating photos with metadata like tags and notes, setting up contacts, and participating in groups. The most notable implicit mechanism is a collaborative filtering in the form "interestingness"—Flickr's own algorithmic means for rating, sorting, and finding photographs. Rather than requiring users to vote, the system dynamically constructs the rating based on an undisclosed formula (secret sauce), based on factors including how many times a photo has been viewed, commented on, marked as favorite, and tagged, as well as who did each action and when. Clusters are another implicit technique based on dynamic analysis of the groups of tag words used together, such as "turkey" with "Istanbul" and "turkey" with "Thanksgiving." Similar to the Google PageRank and AdWords algorithms, the quality of results improve as more people use it, and the system as a whole gains value as a natural byproduct of user behavior.

"Don't build applications. Build contexts for interaction." So, read a slide from Flickr's launch presentation at the O'Reilly Emerging Technology Conference in 2004. The context builds from the basics of online photo storage to integrate identity (customized profiles), circles of trust (family, friends, and contacts), groups, testimonials, discussions, internal messaging systems, and the ability to enforce privacy by blocking unwanted requests. Additionally, a variety of features exist to engage users more deeply in the service through exploration and discovery, including related tags, tag clusters, an Explore page, and recent activity.

Flickr Fans Respond

The *Fast Company* magazine's web site allows users to add comments to stories and for the page featuring an interview with Flickr founder Stewart Butterfield they certainly did. The stream of passionate reader commentary demonstrates just how well the company succeeded in creating the sort of passion that drives viral marketing and growth. "Flickr is an amazing site. It's social software done right, with connections built around content rather than constructed profiles. The money I spent for the Pro account was worth every penny, and I've encouraged most of my friends and family to do the same." "The best thing about Flickr, from a developer's standpoint, is the extensive API." "My favorite aspect of Flickr is that it's easy to get involved in the site, but as you learn more about it, there are several ways to participate and your participation can become quite intense."

The Flickr development team facilitated emergence from the beginning when usage patterns and user feedback led it to evolve its core product from a game platform (originally called Game Never Ending) into a photo-sharing platform. The management and development teams actively solicited feedback through multiple channels, including forums and a blog. This input was fed into Flickr's rapid, sometimes daily, release cycles to evolve the product collaboratively with their customers.

Flickr's marketing budget as it grew from zero to 150,000 users was zero dollars.[91] It leveraged viral network effects like word of mouth, positive reviews in the press, bloggers, and other no-cost mechanisms enabled by the network. Features, like invitations available from every page, make it simple for existing users to virally invite friends and family to use the service. Flickr also uses its own blog, FlickrBlog, as a way for individual members of the Flickr team to become more closely involved with users.

❷ Data Is the Next "Intel Inside"

Flickr is a classic example of a completely user-generated database. It began with a central data element—digital photos—and then invited users to contribute, which offered Flickr a multitude of ways to enhance the core photo data, including metadata like tags and notes, profiles, groups, and discussions. As is so often the case with Web 2.0, network effects amplify the value of these user contributions both inside and outside the service, and the end result is a hard to recreate datasource.

Flickr has been so successful at involving users that more than 85 percent of the photos on its service have human-added metadata.[92] This leaves little doubt that today's Internet users are actively engaged in creating content online and doing so at multiple levels—in this case, ranging from the primary rich media to the supplemental metadata to the photo groups and forums.

To balance users' desire to share their photographs while still maintaining some degree of control over licensing and ownership, Flickr fully integrated the Creative Commons licensing framework[93] into its service. This allows users to make some, but not all, rights reserved by choosing from a range of seven different licensing options, including "None (All Rights Reserved)", "Attribution—Noncommercial" (others can copy and distribute for noncommercial purposes only and must include attribution), and "Attribution—Share Alike" (others may copy and use commercially but must attribute and share their derivative photos under the same terms). As of the second quarter of 2005, more than 1.5 million photos[94] were licensed for reuse using standard technologies like:

- **RSS 2.0 and Atom:** users, including those without Flickr accounts, can subscribe to multiple types of Flickr feeds, including photographs by user, tag, or comments.
- **EXIF**[95] **and IPTC**[96] **image data:** Flickr will display embedded image data for any photograph containing these details.
- **XML:** Flickr API returns XML structured data.
- **Email standards:** users can post photographs to Flickr using standard Internet (SMTP) email with attachments.
- **Blog standards:** users can post photos directly from Flickr to their own blogs. Nine types of blogs are supported, including Blogger, Movable Type, and WordPress, as well as any that support the Atom, Blogger, or MetaWeblog APIs.

Figure 52: Flickr's Blog This feature

The impact of Flickr's strategy on standards support, particularly those for blogs and feeds, is not to be underestimated. Flickr successfully capitalized on the rapid rise in blogging by making its application a very easy-to-use complementary service for bloggers (see Figure 52). Also, Flickr aggregates data in multiple forms to engage its users, including sets, groups, and photostreams. "One Year Ago Today," tag clouds, and interestingness all represent existing data in new ways.

Issues & Debates

Figure 53: Users control who sees their photos

Privacy and data portability are two crucial issues that online services must tackle in the Web 2.0 era. Flickr provides models for both. Although the default sharing for photos is public, users can choose to change this to private levels (e.g., You, Friends, and Family; see Figure 53). Controls allow users to also specify who can comment, download, print, tag, or add notes to their photos (notes and tags default to Contacts only); what types of emails Flickr may send; and granular control over what portions of user profiles are visible. Users can explicitly opt-out of API-based searches. A "Block This Person" feature also allows a user to cut-off Flickr-based interaction from another Flickr user. In terms of data portability, Flickr uses its API to give users full access to data.

❸ Innovation in Assembly

By creating a full-featured API for its service, one that exposes the majority of its application's functionality, Flickr enabled the creation of hundreds of third-party applications. Some applications simply provide alternate user interfaces into its service, while others are sophisticated tools for uploading and managing photographs. As Flickr's Cal Henderson notes, "APIs encourage people to do your work for you," and the process of creating an API is beneficial internally because it "forces clean interfaces" to your service. Flickr has followed a number of API best practices, including:

- **Multiprotocol support.** By supporting three protocols—REST, XML-RPC, and SOAP—Flickr is able to reach a very wide audience of developers, including those looking for lightweight solutions like REST or more structured models like SOAP. The multiple protocols are rationalized into a single code flow to service requests. The API endpoints leverage the same application and business logic as the main web site.

- **Management via developer keys and self-service setup.** To use the service, developers must obtain a developer key (also known as an application key). This model meets the needs of both Flickr and the developers—it is free for the developers and can be obtained immediately via self-service. At the same time, it gives Flickr granular usage tracking, automated developer management, authenticated access, and the ability to control usage such as enforcing adherence to its terms of service.

- **Full documentation.** Flickr offers complete, well-structured documentation with extensive examples and explicit coverage of problem areas such as data and date formats. An API Explorer interface allows experimentation and learning without writing code. It also encourages adoption and reduces support costs.

- **Simplicity.** Flickr's relatively simple API design has several benefits; for example higher rates of adoption across a wider developer base and reduced support costs.

- **Developer support.** A developer's mailing list provides timely cost-effective support and encourages and leverages community contribution.

- **Language kits.** Support for specific programming languages such as Java, .NET, PHP, and Ruby is provided by third-party developers but promoted by Flickr. Support is integrated into developer mailing lists.

Flickr's platform strategy—online photo-sharing application with read–write API, data syndication, external integration, and mobile device support—has enabled it to become the center of a digital-photo ecosystem of partners, third-party applications, mashup developers, and bloggers. Flickr did not try to reinvent the wheel but instead positioned itself as a complement to a range of existing software and services. Even the origin of the API itself, driven by its desire to allow users to export data but not have to build export tools, was strategic. And indeed, once the API was available, customers built tools that Flickr would have otherwise had to build: an iPhoto plugin for Mac OS X, and multiple photo uploaders for Mac, Windows, and even FlickrFS—a virtual filesystem for Linux. This not only saved costs, fostered innovation, and grew market share, it built trust with users.

Flickr is the biggest customer of its own API; for example, its own desktop tool Organizr. By "eating their own dog food" Flickr improves quality, saves development costs, drives quality, and builds the feature set for both itself and its customers. Also, Flickr's photo-based ecosystem builds on a variety of partnerships. For example QOOP offers a print-on-demand photo album creation service, there is one-hour printing through Target, Zazzle for U.S. postage photo stamps, and Englaze for CD and DVD backups. As shown in Figure 54, Flickr seamlessly integrates the print order process into the overall rich user experience.

Figure 54: Flickr's print order process

Much of the Flickr data model is addressable via either URL or its API, including photos, individual blog posts, contacts, favorites, groups, people, comments, and tags. By adopting a strategy of openness, Flickr has fostered customer and partner remixing, which is another factor in contributing to its accelerated growth. The following lists a handful of the hundreds of mashups and tools created:

- **Tools.** Tools include image uploaders for most operating systems, screensavers (Flickr Screensaver), search-and-browse tools (Flickr Search Plugin and FlickrStorm), and album creation (Flickr Album Maker).

- **Commercial services.** Besides services like QOOP, Zazzle, and Englaze, the unique characteristics of Flickr—photostreams, groups, etc.—can lead to similarly unique third-party services like Moo, which offers members a way to create mini business cards from their photos and data.

- **Maps integration.** After Yahoo!'s purchase of Flickr, Yahoo! Maps was integrated into Flickr directly. Earlier tools included GeoBloggers.com, which used metadata embedded in photos to automatically plot images on Google Maps.

- **Photo games and toys.** Creative developers have created dozens of photo-based games, including Flickr Sudoku for photo-puzzles and Fastr, a photo guessing game. fd's Flickr Toys has more than 20 small utility applications for manipulating Flickr photos.

When you introduce an API, you must be prepared to handle the impact from users applying it in ways you didn't anticipate. For example, Flickr encountered the following scenario: a developer wrote a great Flickr photo screensaver, thousands of people downloaded it, and it hits the Flickr servers every two seconds, which creates an excessive load.[97] Possible solutions included extensive caching on the server side (which aids both the API and the production site) and application/developer keys combined with system monitoring to enforce policy.

❹ Rich User Experiences

Since its inception, Flickr focused on creating a sophisticated user experience designed to combine the best aspects of the desktop and the Web. It has progressively refined and enhanced its product by incrementally adding features while maintaining an uncluttered, user-focused interface. Immediate in-context editing of images, tags, and comments, using techniques like Ajax, provide more desktop-like interactivity without requiring slow page reloads (see Figure 55).

Flickr matches its technology to the objective user experience by avoiding a one-size-fits-all philosophy. Besides using an earlier hybrid Flash–Ajax model, Flickr and partners provided desktop tools to improve user efficiency for some tasks (e.g., Organizr from Flickr and iPhoto plugin). Flickr's initial implementation relied heavily on Adobe Flash technology, but has progressively moved to a more Ajax-centric approach over time. One key benefit of moving from Flash to Ajax is easier addressability of content simplifying basic tasks like direct linking to images.

Creating platform-specific desktop applications can be a costly proposition. Flickr has attempted to balance the user needs for sophisticated rich media management on the one hand and fully browser-based, platform-agnostic tools on the other. Flickr's approach lets users do what they need on whatever platform they find convenient.

❺ Software Above the Level of a Single Device

Flickr's service is built to span devices, desktops, and networks. This is fundamental to its long-term success, given that, as of the second quarter of 2006, more than 300 million cameraphones were in use and have grown 75 percent per year. In 2006, more than 1 billion photos will be taken from phones. An estimated 10 percent of the photos on Flickr were directly uploaded from mobile devices.

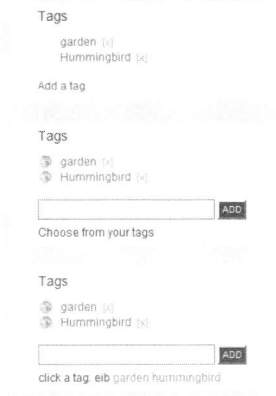

Figure 55: *Ajax features incorporated into Flickr*

Customers have many ways to upload images directly to Flickr from their mobile phones and other handheld devices, but, thanks to its API, Flickr did not build any of them. Third parties, both companies and individuals, gladly did this work. Both software providers and enterprise IT organizations often fail to reach this large, growing population out of fear—fear of the diversity of mobile platforms and the inherent development costs and support complexities. Flickr leveraged the network to support the network. For example, by using Shozu, cameraphone users can send photos to Flickr with a single click. zipPhoto provides this capability for Microsoft Smartphone and Pocket PC users. Flickr works on other edge devices as well. A third-party developer used Flickr's API to create an application that retrieves Flickr photos for display on a TiVo device. Flickr does not serve the same images to mobile devices as desktops—small screen devices typically get thumbnails less than 100 pixels wide and 5K in size.[98]

❻ Perpetual Beta

In Flickr's early days it released not only often, but very often—multiple releases per day were not unusual. Three essential development process guidelines helped ensure this rapid release model worked: source code control, a one-step-build process, and bug-tracking software.[99]

Flickr built to scale by adopting a horizontal architecture based on low-cost commodity hardware and open source software.[100] This architectural strategy let it start small and incrementally add more servers as the customer base rapidly grew (at 30 percent per month) into millions of users. Contrast this with the costly and risky dot-com era strategy of vertical scaling by relying on big expensive hardware with significantly greater upfront investment and less ongoing flexibility. Flickr also managed cost and complexity by avoiding unnecessary textbook infrastructure, such as an application tier, and instead focused on what was most important to its specific application—web servers, storage servers, and database servers—all geared toward flexible, high-performance image and data retrieval.

Application instrumentation was also critical to Flickr's success. It tracked usage carefully and created internal dashboards,[101] including types of shadow applications, such as its home-grown "Loneliest User" utility.

Flickr uses the PHP dynamic scripting language for the bulk of its service, including application logic, page logic, templates, and the API. This language choice facilitated agile, lightweight development processes, which allowed quick responses to changing requirements and customer feedback. In contrast to earlier preconceptions about the scalability of scripting languages, Flickr was able to serve more than 1,000 pages per second (the database delivering more than 25,000 transactions per second). Note that Flickr did not rely on a single language alone—Java was used for specific back-end functionality, and JavaScript, Flash, and other frontend technologies were used to create a rich user experience.

❼ Leveraging the Long Tail

From sign-up through the entire product use cycle, Flickr provides a wide range of self-service tools for customers. A thorough "Your account" page allows users to manage profiles, privacy settings, photos, and other settings. Setup and management of developer accounts for the API is also self-service based, and support forums provide a peer-based mechanism for knowledge sharing (the Flickr staff contributes as well).

Flickr facilitates aggregation, filtering, and search, beginning with its role as aggregator of photos for millions of photographers. An internal search engine supports filtering and search, while discovery and exploration are facilitated by an architecture of participation techniques like tags, the interestingness filter, and groups. External search, the findability of Flickr content from anywhere on the Internet, is enhanced by Flickr's adoption of search engine optimization techniques such as clean, easy to read URLs.

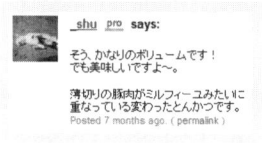

Figure 56: Capturing the global market

A significant percentage of Flickr's customer base comes from outside the United States. By supporting internationalization standards, such as Unicode's UTF-8 character format, it was able to better capture this global market (see Figure 56). The read–write nature of Web 2.0 and user-generated content demands that applications behind online services be fully internationalized not only for information display, but for input as well.

❽ Lightweight Models and Cost-Effective Scalability

At the time of its acquisition by Yahoo!, Flickr had more than 250,000 customers, was growing at a rate of 30 percent per month, and had a staff of only 11 employees.

Syndication is crucial to Flickr's success. For example, by offering a basic free account and comprehensive support for the major blogging platforms, Flickr quickly became the preferred choice for a growing army of active bloggers, who could easily plug into the site and workflow. And, of course, many of those same users became paying Pro Account users.

Flickr would not have succeeded if not for the ways in which it leveraged the new IT economics of Web 2.0. Flickr's:

- Offices were in Vancouver, British Columbia, but its infrastructure was in Texas and Virginia—outsourced hosting is now the default option.

- Software platform is built on a classic LAMP stack: Linux operating system, Apache web server, MySQL database, and PHP, as well as open source infrastructure tools like Cacti and Ganglia.

- Servers are low-cost, commodity PCs. Flickr offers a multichannel and scaled multitier revenue model:

    — Advertising: Contextual advertising

    — Premium accounts: Flickr Pro Accounts at $24.95/year with unlimited storage, full-resolution images, and no advertising.

    — Partnerships: Target for photo print services and QOOP for photo books and posters.

In the first quarter of 2006, Flickr was storing more than 2 million photos consuming 368 TBs of storage. Just a few years ago this would have been economically impractical due to the storage costs alone. The 73 percent decrease over the last six years makes this a feasible business model.

Web 2.0 vs. 1.0: Flickr vs. Shutterfly

During Flickr's rapid rise, it stood in stark contrast to more traditional online photo services like Shutterfly. By emphasizing the social aspects of photography, Flickr captured market share through network effects created via public sharing, comments, groups, and other techniques. In the online photo market it introduced new ideas like subscribing to photos as RSS feeds (syndication), the use of user-defined tags (folksonomies), emergent navigation and recommendations (collaborative filtering), as well as browser-centric rich user interface techniques like Ajax. Some of these distinctions remain, although Shutterfly has subsequently adopted many of the techniques Flickr pioneered. Flickr's acquisition by Yahoo! in 2005 and Shutterfly's IPO in 2006 move the competition to a new level (see Figure 57).

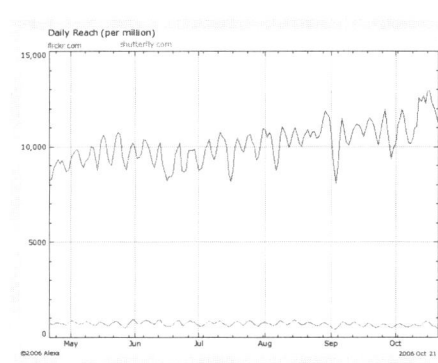

Figure 57: Flickr vs. Shutterfly Alexa rankings

Controlling the Wisdom of Crowds at Flickr

Flickr provides a "Report Abuse" option, which gives users a means for policing their community when other members have violated the terms of use or community guidelines. Flickr's terms of service outlines its privacy policy, member conduct, and other legal policies and guidelines. For example, every photo page gives users the ability to "Flag this photo as 'may offend.'" Over time, Flickr has had to modify the algorithms for its interestingness ratings to counteract people trying to game the system. Founder Stewart Butterfield noted that once users discovered that adding a photo to multiple groups impacted the rating, an "arms race" began. Photos were added to progressively larger numbers of groups, sometimes up to 70 groups for a single photo.

SECTION IV

Web 2.0 Assessment

Having identified the core best practices of Web 2.0 and understanding how others have applied them is a valuable prerequisite to the true test—the ability to apply these best practices to your own enterprise. The following structured questionnaire will guide you through this process of:

- Assessing your organization and products in relation to Web 2.0 best practices
- Identifying gaps, risks, and opportunities for improvement
- Formulating a strategy and plan for leveraging Web 2.0 techniques to better meet your organizational and product objectives

This model can be applied to both existing and planned products as well as to internally and externally facing applications. The structure of the questionnaire is based on the eight core patterns of Web 2.0. They can be reviewed in sequence or independently. Keep in mind some general adoption guidelines:

Learn

- Start with this report and the Web 2.0 Reading List of best web sites and books
    - Use a simple tool like Bloglines to subscribe to a set of relevant blogs for your industry and interests as well as some Web 2.0-specific blogs
- Get firsthand experience using a variety of Web 2.0 applications
    - Use del.icio.us for bookmarks and Flickr for photos, create a blog using Blogger or Live Spaces, create a LinkedIn profile, and try YouTube
- See where Web 2.0 is impacting your industry, partners, competitors, and customers
    - Do any of your competitors apply practices from this report?
    - Are there any startups trying to disrupt the status quo?

Plan

- Evaluate where Web 2.0 patterns and practices align with your needs
    - Use this assessment as input
- Establish a plan with both short and longer-term objectives
    - Consider by functional area (marketing, operations, etc.) or class of objective (increase revenue and decrease costs)
- Begin staff training on appropriate technologies, products, or processes
    - Whether it's a small team or group, clear objectives are crucial

Pilot

- Start with pilot projects
- Incrementally change processes, tools, and strategy
- Establish measures for success or failure

Execute and evolve

- Gradually incorporate core attributes of Web 2.0 (simple, open, user-centered)
- Suit to fit: don't adopt a technique or strategy because it is in vogue
- Use defined metrics to determine where Web 2.0-related efforts are effective
- Maintain perspective: it is not an all-or-nothing proposition
- Change in Web 2.0 is driven as much by nontechnical factors, if not more, than technical ones
- Iterate and refine

Harnessing Collective Intelligence

How many steps does it take for a new user to sign-up for your service?

- If it is more than one page, how can it be simplified?
- Are all "required fields" really required?
- Can customers use the service immediately after signup?
- Is there an evaluation option, or, even better, a base-level free account model that allows prospective customers to use the service before requiring payment?

Do you pay the user first by minimizing barriers to accessing your service's primary function?

- How many steps does this process take?
- Can users access this from the home page (or their home page)? Or via an always-available menu or other navigation?
- Does your system learn from past user behavior to make repeat actions simpler? Can you prepopulate or suggest values to speed data entry?
- Do prerequisites or dependencies exist before a user can begin using your service? If so, can these be mitigated? For example, if a client-side download is required, can a browser-based equivalent be provided?

Have you identified where network effects can be leveraged within your application or service?

- How do you explicitly encourage network effects?
- Do you set network effects by default?
- Do you have an "Invite Others" option or comparable mechanism to encourage adoption?
- What mechanisms allow users to make connections to others within the system?
- Can users form or join groups?
- Is viral adoption part of your marketing strategy?

What, if any, forms of user-contributed content, user feedback, metadata is supported?

- If you don't have any of these options, where can they be added to provide the most value?
- How successful have they been?

What incentives do you provide for users to contribute and participate?

- Where can they be added or improved?
- How do you measure the success of these incentives?

What implicit techniques do you use to harness collective intelligence?

- Are there collaborative filtering techniques that may be appropriate?
- Can users refine the filtering criteria?

As more customers use the application and how does it improve?

- Does your system adapt or learn from user behavior in any way?
- Is aggregate user behavior and data leveraged?

Does navigation or data findability automatically improve based on the data set or user behavior?

Where can Web 2.0 patterns and practices improve "feedback loops" between you and your partners and customers?

Do you have an established corporate policy on employee blogging?

How aware are you of what is being said about your company in the blogosphere, on product review sites, and comparable venues?

- Which groups within your organization are, or should be, responsible for this?

What hierarchical data (taxonomy) could benefit from the addition of folksonomic (user-added) classification?

What controls and quality guards are in place to regulate user activity?

- Are the appropriate policy and Terms of Use available and up to date?
- Are feedback forms or more specific abuse-prevention mechanisms in place?

What privacy controls do you have in place for user-contributed data and content?

- Do you explicitly state your privacy policy to users?
- Can users control which information is available to whom?

> *Data Is the Next "Intel Inside"*

What data sets give you a competitive advantage?

- How are they leveraged through your online services?
- What are the obstacles to implementing these data sets (legal, cost, proprietary advantage)?

Are users given the ability to enhance existing data?

- How do you measure the success of these capabilities?
- Where would this enhance the value of the application?

Do you have a data stack strategy?

- Is third-party data currently incorporated as part of your offerings, or is your data part of partner or customer stacks?

How is data collected online?

- Do you collect user information such as behavioral data, user-generated content, aggregate user metrics?
- How is this leveraged within your business: marketing strategy, product strategy, and customer relationship/lifecycle management?

In what industry standard formats is your data available?

- Are there additional formats—XML, RSS, iCal, OPML, microformats—that if provided could create new opportunities or increase reach?

To what extent is your service a walled garden?

- What are the tradeoffs to this strategy?

If users create or store their own data—either rich media or structured information—do you give them a mechanism to export that data?

- Are there suitable industry-standard formats for this operation?

What licensing policy applies to any user-contributed content?

- Are users given the ability to specify a licensing option?
- Is a Creative Commons or comparable model appropriate?
- Is your policy on this topic oriented toward maximizing viral adoption? (That is, favoring minimal restrictions on reuse.)
- If legal or compliance considerations influence your current strategy, how do these manifest, and what modifications might improve chances for product success?

Innovation in Assembly

In what ways does your product and service support remixing?

Do you support content syndication?

- Which of your constituencies could benefit? For example, users (content updates, product notifications), press/PR (press releases), investors (IR), developers (platform updates), recruiting (job notifications), and internal (HR/corporate notifications).
- Is your content aggregated by third-party services?
- What syndication data formats do you support?

Do you offer external APIs to your service?

- What areas of your application would benefit from exposing an API?
- What constituencies leverage an API? Partners? Third-party application or tool providers? Independent developers and general public?
- Do your competitors offer or plan to offer APIs?
- How do you measure success for your APIs?
- Are your APIs directly tied to revenue (e.g., Amazon and eBay)?
- Do you charge for usage? What limits do you have in place?
- What elements of a developer-support program do you have in place (e.g., community, forums, blogs or wikis)?
- What API best practices do you follow? Versioning? Developer or application IDs?
- Can users sign-up for APIs via self-service?

Where do you or can you use your own API?

- In what scenarios could benefits be shared by your teams and external developers?

Do you use APIs or otherwise build on online services from other providers?

How do you monitor and track how customers are remixing your services and data?

- Do you reward customers for innovation?
- How do customer innovations via your platform feed back into your product or strategy?

At what level of granularity is your content available?

- Besides traditional web pages, how else is your data available online?
- If you delivered data in smaller chunks, could that enable new forms of remixing and potential new revenue streams?
- Do you support microformats?
- How well structured and clean is the URL design of your service?

Enterprise questions include:

- If you have an SOA, how can it benefit from the technologies and techniques of Web 2.0, including RSS, REST, and Ajax?
- Where can existing and planned composite applications, dashboards, and intranets benefit from external web service components and APIs?
- Where can SaaS help you lower costs by increasing your operational efficiency?
- Can you extend existing collaboration tools, including Exchange and Notes, with plug-in capabilities from Web 2.0-type third-party tools and services?

Rich User Experiences

How and where do your online products and services integrate the best of online and desktop experiences?

- Have you identified where this would be appropriate?

Which, if any, of the rich interface techniques and tools do you use (e.g., Ajax or Flash)?

Have you evaluated open source and vendor-supported Ajax toolkits?

Have you evaluated new Flash tools such as Flex and Apollo?

How does your application personalize the experience for each user?

- Which elements of this are user-specified and which happen automatically?

Software Above the Level of a Single Device

How does your product or service go beyond the desktop browser?

- Is there a strategy in place for doing so?
- What areas have been most or least successful?

What non-desktop scenarios can increase your product's reach or market share?

- Are there complementary services or partnerships for these cases?
- What are the greatest obstacles to moving in this direction?

Are there any location-aware uses for your product?

What other Web 2.0 practices can you apply to reach mobile and edge devices or to improve your existing mobile offerings?

- An architecture of participation that can benefit from greater reach?
- An extensible platform strategy?
- Ability to capture more of the Long Tail?

If you have non-desktop user experiences, how can they be improved?

- Can they use a more effective, streamlined user experience?

What data-location independence issues do you or your customers face?

- Is synchronizing data across locations or devices an issue you can address?
- How can you simplify data access?

What digital home opportunities exist for your product and services?

What technology standards do you leverage as part of your mobile device strategy?

Perpetual Beta

What is the length of your typical product release cycle?

- How can you shorten this interval?
- What are your barriers to a "release early, release often" development mode?

Do you have the tools and processes in place to support rapid release cycles (e.g., rigorous source code control, nightly builds, accurate defect tracking, deployment tools)?

How do you engage users as real-time testers?

- Are all product feature decisions made in-advance and on paper?
- Do you perform live A/B testing?
- Do you have a metrics program in place to evaluate the effectiveness of new product features?

Do you currently consider operations to be a core competency?

- What performance and uptime metrics do you track?

Do you incrementally roll-out new products?

- Do all products go through a private beta phase?

In what ways do you instrument your online services?

- What in-house tools have you built to support your online applications?

What dynamic tools and languages do you use?

Leveraging the Long Tail

Which of the Long Tail's democratizing forces apply to your business—production tools, distribution and aggregation, or search and filtering?

Have the economics of the Long Tail impacted your industry?

- Are any niche micromarkets for your products and services becoming more economically viable?

List the ways in which your site explicitly matches supply and demand?

- Are algorithmic techniques such as collaborative filtering applied?
- Is an individual customer history used to improve or tailor the online experience?

- Does your site "learn" over time from both individual and aggregate behavior?
- Do you have metrics in place to track the impact of these methods?

What data filtering and search mechanisms do you provide?

- Is a search box available on every page of your site?

How does your product or service capitalize on the costs of operating online?

- Can you identify specifics in marketing, sales, and support?

What types of customer self-service does your application and service provide?

- What cost-savings or market-expanding opportunities might this enable?

Lightweight Models and Cost-Effective Scalability

List the ways in which your business or product is designed to scale with demand

- What is the technology scaling strategy?

Have you taken advantage of any other syndicated business models?

- Are there revenue- or cost-savings opportunities for you do so?

What aspects of your business can be syndicated online?

- Are there appropriate affiliate models?
- Is there opportunity for a widget model for pluggable integration?

Where have you outsourced infrastructure, function, or expertise?

- If not, what are the obstacles to doing so?

Are there functions or core competencies of your product or business that can become an outsourced component for others?

Do you have a scalable pricing and revenue model?

- Do you offer a free service as a way to drive adoption?
- In what ways can you offer partial or scaled-down services for free or lower cost?

Are there untapped revenue models for your online offerings, such as advertising (either via syndication or sponsorship) or subscriptions, transaction commissions, or premium services?

APPENDIX A
Web 2.0 Reading List

Web 2.0 General

Books/Articles/Readings

Christenson, Clayton, *The Innovator's Dilemma*, Collins

O'Reilly, Tim, "What Is Web 2.0?", *http://www.oreillynet.com/pub/a/oreilly/tim/news/2005/09/30/what-is-web-20.html*

O'Reilly, Tim, *The Open Source Paradigm Shift*, *http://tim.oreilly.com/opensource*

Raymond, Eric S., *The Cathedral and the Bazaar*, O'Reilly, *http://www.oreilly.com/catalog/cb*

Web Sites/Blogs

O'Reilly Radar, *http://radar.oreilly.com*

TechCrunch, *http://www.techcrunch.com*

Web 2.0 Workgroup, *http://www.web20workgroup.com*

Events

Web 2.0 Conference, *http://www.web2con.com*

Web 2.0 Expo, *http://web2expo.com*

Harnessing Collective Intelligence

Books/Articles/Readings

Bricklin, Dan, "The Cornucopia of the Commons: How to Get Volunteer Labor" *http://www.bricklin.com/cornucopia.htm*

Garret, Jesse James, "An Interview with Flickr's Eric Costello", *http://adaptivepath.com/publications/essays/archives/000519.php*

Lessig, Lawrence, *Code and Other Laws of Cyberspace*, Basic Books

O'Reilly, Tim, "The Open Source Paradigm Shift", *http://tim.oreilly.com/articles/paradigmshift_0504.html*

Shirkey, Clay, "Ontology Is Overrated: Categories, Links, and Tags", *http://www.shirky.com/writings/ontology_overrated.html*

Web Sites/Blogs

Mashable, *http://www.mashable.com*

Read/Write Web, *http://www.readwriteweb.com*

Data Is the Next "Intel Inside"

Books/Articles/Readings

O'Reilly, Tim, "Open Data: Small Pieces Loosely Joined", *http://radar.oreilly.com/archives/2006/09/a_platform_beats_an_applicatio.html*

Web Sites/Blogs

MicroContent Musings, *http://www.sivas.com/microcontent/musings/blog*

Microformats, *http://microformats.org*

Innovation in Assembly

Books/Articles/Readings

Bausch, Paul and Bumgardner, Jim, *Flickr Hacks*, O'Reilly, *http://www.oreilly.com/catalog/flickrhks*

Henderson, Cal, *Building Scalable Web Sites*, O'Reilly, *http://www.oreilly.com/catalog/web2apps*

Torkington, Nathan, "How to Roll Out an Open API", *http://radar.oreilly.com/archives/2005/05/web_services_es.html*

Gibson, Rich and Erle, Schuyler, *Google Maps Hacks*, O'Reilly, *http://www.oreilly.com/catalog/googlemapshks*

Web Sites/Blogs

ProgrammableWeb, *http://www.programmableweb.com*

Software as Services, *http://blogs.zdnet.com/SAAS*

Events

Mashup Camp, *http://www.mashupcamp.com*

Software Above the Level of a Single Device

Books/Articles/Readings

Stutz, David, "Advice to Microsoft Regarding Commodity Software", *http://www.synthesist.net/writing/onleavingms.html*

Web Sites/Blogs

GigaOM, *http://www.gigaom.com*

Open Gardens, *http://opengardensblog.futuretext.com*

Rich User Experiences	*Books/Articles/Readings*
	Gehtland, Justin, Galbraith, Ben, and Almaer, Dion, *Pragmatic Ajax,* Pragmatic Programmers, *http://www.oreilly.com/catalog/0976694085*
	Mahemoff, Michael, *Ajax Design Patterns*, O'Reilly, *http://www.oreilly.com/catalog/ajaxdp*
	McLaughlin, Brett, *Head Rush Ajax*, O'Reilly, *http://www.oreilly.com/catalog/headra*
	Web Sites/Blogs
	Ajax Patterns, *http://ajaxpatterns.org*
	Ajaxian, *http://www.ajaxian.com*
	Events
	AJAXWorld, *http://www.ajaxworldexpo.com*
Leveraging the Long Tail	*Books/Articles/Readings*
	Anderson, Chris, "The Long Tail", *Wired*, *http://www.wired.com/wired/archive/12.10/tail.html*
	Anderson, Chris, *The Long Tail: Why the Future of Business Is Selling Less of More*, Hyperion
	Web Sites/Blogs
	The Long Tail, *http://www.longtail.com*
Lightweight Models and Cost-Effective Scalability	*Books/Articles/Readings*
	37signals, "Getting Real", *https://gettingreal.37signals.com*
	Web Sites/Blogs
	Signal vs. Noise, *http://www.37signals.com/svn*
Enterprise 2.0	*Books/Articles/Readings*
	McAfee, Andrew P., "Enterprise 2.0: The Dawn of Emergent Collaboration", *MIT Sloan Management Review*, Spring 2006, Vol. 47, No. 3, pp. 21–28, *http://sloanreview.mit.edu/smr/issue/2006/spring/06*
	Web Sites/Blogs
	Dion Hinchcliffe's Enterprise Web 2.0, *http://blogs.zdnet.com/Hinchcliffe*
	Andrew McAfee, *http://blog.hbs.edu/faculty/amcafee*

APPENDIX B

Technologies of Web 2.0

Although implementing Web 2.0 best practices is fundamentally much more about technique than technology, there are some newer technologies that can play an important role. Web 2.0 builds on all the open standards that have made the Web so successful: TCP/IP, HTTP, HTML, MIME, URLs, XML, and the rest of the core Internet technologies and protocols of the past 30 years. Therefore, take this list in context and remember that none of the following are required, but use as appropriate for each unique set of requirements.

Technologies

- **Really Simple Syndication (RSS).** An XML text-based data format containing a list of items, each typically with a title, summary, URL link, and date (some additional data is optional). RSS, when published, is often referred to as a syndicated feed. Users subscribe to feeds using feed readers or aggregators that can be web-based or desktop applications. Multiple versions of RSS exist. Operating system providers, such as Microsoft via Windows Vista, are now integrating RSS support directly at the OS level. Many types of information are commonly published in RSS (such as blog and news data) but the simplicity and utility of RSS are leading to much more widespread usage. For example, del.icio.us lets users subscribe to bookmarks added for any subject or by any person; Flickr lets customers subscribe to another person's photostream. Microsoft CTO Ray Ozzie sees "using RSS as a DNA of sorts to enable 'mesh' information sharing…RSS has the potential to be the 'Unix pipe of the Internet.'"[102] See also:

    — All About RSS, *http://faganfinder.com/search/rss.shtml*

    — Wikipedia: *http://en.wikipedia.org/wiki/RSS_(file_format)*

- **Atom.** A more recent XML-based data syndication format intended to provide greater structure and XML standards compliance than RSS. Atom 1.0 became an IETF standard in 2005 as RFC 4287. Ongoing debate exists between advocates of RSS (simplicity) and Atom (features), although most tools for XML-based syndication support both formats. There is also an Atom Publishing Protocol (APP) that allows publishing and editing web resources using Atom-formatted XML over HTTP. Google has recently begun building on Atom and RSS as part of its "GData" protocol.[103] See also:

    — IEFT RFC 4287, *http://tools.ietf.org/html/rfc4287*

- **Microformats.** A set of XHTML extensions for expressing greater semantic meaning within web pages. Microformat standards exist for common concepts including people (hCard), events (hCalendar), and reviews (hReview). They often build on existing standards, such as hCalendar, which implements the iCalendar standard (RFC 2445) in semantic XHTML. Vendors have begun applying microformats: Yahoo! Local (hCalendar and hCard), Yahoo! Shopping (hReview), Technorati (rel-tag), and Upcoming.org (hCard). See also:

    — *http://microformats.org*

    — Using Microformats, *http://www.oreilly.com/catalog/microformats*

Applications

- **Blogs.** A "web log" is a form of web publishing characterized by a series of entries or posts, that are typically presented as a list in reverse chronological order. Posts can be viewed individually by a permalink URL assigned to each post. Blogs facilitate decentralized conversations by allowing readers to add comments to posts, as well as tracking when one blog refers to a post in another blog (known as a trackback). Typically written by one or more authors, or bloggers, and managed through the use of blog server applications. Blog content is typically syndicated as feeds via the RSS or Atom XML formats, and read by users via feed aggregators (see RSS entry). See also:

    — *http://en.wikipedia.org/wiki/Blog*

- **Wikis.** Wikis are web sites that allow users to freely add and update pages directly from a web browser. They are often created and maintained as collaborative efforts. The name comes from the Hawaiian phrase "wiki wiki" meaning quick and was first invented by Ward Cunningham in the mid 1990s. Ward has described a wiki as the "simplest online database that could possibly work." The best known wiki is the online encyclopedia project Wikipedia. Both open source and commercial wiki software is available. Commercial products include Socialtext and JotSpot.

Programming Languages/Platforms/Techniques

- **Apollo.** Still in Adobe labs, Apollo is an OS-independent runtime that allows developers to build desktop applications using both Flash and Ajax.

- **Ajax.** Ajax a set of techniques for creating richer and more responsive web applications. It builds on standards and technologies that have matured over the Web's first decade, including XHTML and CSS, the Document Object Model (DOM), XML, and XSLT, as well as JavaScript. Ajax techniques can reduce or eliminate the slow click-and-wait interactions that characterized earlier generations of web applications. The term Ajax itself was coined by Jesse James Garret in early 2005.

- **Flex.** Adobe's family of products for creating RIA in the browser using Flash.
- **Linux, Apache, MySQL and Perl, PHP, and Python (LAMP).** A set of popular open source software that is often used to build and run web sites. Although available independently, together they provide a well-integrated stack—operating system, web server, database, and dynamic programming language. Benefits include low cost (typically free), wide support, and scalability. Many of the Web 2.0 exemplars in this report run on a variation of the LAMP stack. See also:
    - *http://www.onlamp.com*
- **Web services.** Standardized ways of integrating distributed applications on top of Internet-based protocols and data formats. One of web services biggest benefits is that they allow applications to communicate independently of operating system, programming language, and location. During the past few years, a variety of standards have been introduced to support web services including Simple Object Access Protocol (SOAP, a transport mechanism), Web Services Description Language (WSDL, for services description), and Universal Description, Discovery and Integration (UDDI, for services registry and lookup). Most web services rely on eXtensible Markup Language (XML) for data structure. See also:
    - *http://webservices.xml.com*
    - *http://www.w3.org/2002/ws*
- **Service oriented architecture (SOA).** A software architecture model for building loosely coupled distributed systems. It typically refers to intra-enterprise IT system and builds on top of web services technologies and designs. A more recent set of standards have been adopted or proposed as a way to support more the complex requirements of these systems including security (WS-Security), transactions (WS-Transactions), and messaging (WS-Notification). Collectively these are sometimes referred to as WS-*.
- **Representational State Transfer (REST).** An architectural style for web services. Roy Fielding, one of the authors of the original HTTP specification, defined the term in his doctoral dissertation in 2000 but the style itself—essentially how the Web is designed to work—pre-dates the paper. Note that REST is a style, not a standard. It is characterized by a pull-based client-server design, stateless operation, resources named via clean URLs and the core HTTP methods of GET, POST, PUT, and DELETE are used to model the essential REST operations (interfaces). In Web 2.0 the simplicity of this approach is often contrasted with simpler approaches such as REST. See also:
    - *http://www.ics.uci.edu/~fielding/pubs/dissertation/top.htm*
- **Ruby on Rails.** An open source framework for rapid web application development written in the Ruby programming language. Originally created in 2003 by 37signals' David Heinemeier Hansson as the foundation for its Basecamp product suite, "Rails" quickly gained a strong following. The framework encourages an agile, lightweight development style that builds on Ruby's strengths as an object-oriented scripting language, and it has tight Ajax integration that simplifies building sophisticated web-based applications. Subsequently, it inspired similar frameworks in other languages such as Django for Python.

Endnotes

1. "One Billion People Online!", eMarketer, May 18, 2006
   http://www.emarketer.com/eStatDatabase/ArticlePreview.aspx?1003975

2. "Global Technology/Internet Trends", Mary Meeker, Morgan Stanley, November 15, 2005
   http://www.morganstanley.com/institutional/techresearch/gsb112005.html

3. "China Set to Be the Number One Broadband Market by 2007", Ovum, September 6, 2006
   http://www.ovum.com/go/content/c,377,66667

4. "Xu Jinglei Most Popular blogger in World", *China Daily,* August 24, 2006,
   http://www.chinadaily.com.cn/china/2006-08/24/content_672747.htm

5. Horrigan, John B., "Home Broadband Adoption 2006", Pew Internet & American Life Project, May 28, 2006, page 10,
   http://www.pewinternet.org/pdfs/PIP_Broadband_trends2006.pdf

6. Horrigan, John B., "Home Broadband Adoption 2006", Pew Internet & American Life Project, May 28, 2006,
   http://www.pewinternet.org/pdfs/PIP_Broadband_trends2006.pdf

7. Horrigan, John B., "Home Broadband Adoption 2006", Pew Internet & American Life Project, May 28, 2006, page 2,
   http://www.pewinternet.org/pdfs/PIP_Broadband_trends2006.pdf

8. Horrigan, John B., Pew Internet & American Life Project, "Home Broadband Adoption 2006", page 11,
   http://www.pewinternet.org/pdfs/PIP_Broadband_trends2006.pdf

9. Horrigan, John B., "Home Broadband Adoption 2006", Pew Internet & American Life Project, May 28, 2006,
   http://www.pewinternet.org/pdfs/PIP_Broadband_trends2006.pdf

10. "Worldwide Cellular Connections Exceeds 2 Billion", GSM World News, September 15, 2005,
    http://www.gsmworld.com/news/press_2005/press05_21.shtml

11. Ipsos Research, "Mobile Phones Could Soon Rival the PC As World's Dominant Internet Platform", April 18, 2006,
    http://www.ipsos-na.com/news/pressrelease.cfm?id=3049

12. A. T. Kearney/University of Cambridge—Judge Institute of Management, October 2005 (via eMarketer)

13. Horrigan, John B., "Home Broadband Adoption 2006", Pew Internet & American Life Project, May 28, 2006, page 10,
    http://www.pewinternet.org/pdfs/PIP_Broadband_trends2006.pdf

14. Horrigan, John B., "Home Broadband Adoption 2006", Pew Internet & American Life Project, May 28, 2006, pg. 13,
    http://www.pewinternet.org/pdfs/PIP_Broadband_trends2006.pdf

15. ibid

16 Sifry, David, "State of the Blogosphere, August 2006",
    http://www.sifry.com/alerts/archives/000436.html

17 Gonsalves, Antone, "Social Networks Attract Nearly Half of All Web Users", *InformationWeek,* May 2006,
    http://www.informationweek.com/showArticle.jhtml?articleID=187202878

18 Reiss, Spencer, "His Space", *Wired,* July 2006
    http://www.wired.com/wired/archive/14.07/murdoch.html

19 "YouTube: Waiting for The Payoff", *BusinessWeek,* September 18, 2006
    http://www.businessweek.com/magazine/content/06_38/b4001074.htm?chan=tc&campaign_id=bier_tcs.g3a.rss090806b

20 "Craigslist Mulling Fees for Boston Postings", *Boston Business Journal,* February 6, 2006,
    http://boston.bizjournals.com/boston/stories/2006/02/06/daily2.html

21 Pew Internet & American Life Project: Internet Adoption,
    http://www.pewinternet.org/PPF/r/148/report_display.asp

22 Kraus, Joe, "It's a Great Time to Be an Entrepreneur", June 29, 2005,
    http://bnoopy.typepad.com/bnoopy/2005/06/its_a_great_tim.html

23 Electronic Computer Price Index, Bureau of Labor Statistics,
    http://data.bls.gov

24 Internet Advertising Bureau, Advertising Revenue Report, October 2006
    http://www.iab.net/resources/adrevenue/pdf/IAB_PwC%202006Q2.pdf

25 Internet Advertising Bureau, Advertising Revenue Report, October 2006, page 5,
    http://www.iab.net/resources/adrevenue/pdf/IAB_PwC%202006Q2.pdf

26 Berners-Lee, Tim, "So I Have a Blog", December 12, 2005,
    http://dig.csail.mit.edu/breadcrumbs/node/38

27 Metcalfe, Robert, "Metcalfe's Law Recurses Down the Long Tail of Social Networks", August 18, 2006,
    http://vcmike.wordpress.com/2006/08/18/metcalfe-social-networks

28 Reed, David P., "That Sneaky Exponential—Beyond Metcalfe's Law to the Power of Community Building",
    http://www.reed.com/Papers/GFN/reedslaw.html

29 Dan Bricklin, "Cornucopia of the Commons: How to Get Volunteer Labor",
    http://www.bricklin.com/cornucopia.htm

30 Wikipedia statistics as of January 2006,
    http://en.wikipedia.org/wiki/Wikipedia:Statistics

31 Stewart, Sharla A., "Can Behavioral Economics Save Us from Ourselves?", *University of Chicago Magazine,* February 2005, http://magazine.uchicago.edu/0502/features/economics.shtml

32 Lohr, Steve, " New Microsoft Browser Raises Google's Hackles", *New York Times,* May 1, 2006, http://www.nytimes.com/2006/05/01/technology/01google.html

33 Rivlin, Gary, "Wallflower at the Web Party", *New York Times,* October 15, 2006 http://www.nytimes.com/2006/10/15/business/yourmoney/15friend.html

34 Breslau, Karen, "10 Big Thinkers for Big Business", *Newsweek,* June 13, 2006, http://www.msnbc.msn.com/id/8101335/site/newsweek

35 Courtney, Jim, "eBay, PayPal, Skype by the Numbers", *Skype Journal,* June 18, 2006, http://www.skypejournal.com/blog/archives/2006/06/ebay_paypal_skype_by_the_numbers.php

36 Marks, Paul, "Pentagon Sets Its Sights on Social Networking Websites", *New Scientist,* June 9, 2006, http://www.newscientist.com/article/mg19025556.200?DCMP=NLC-nletter&nsref=mg19025556.200

37 Cook, John, "Beware of What You Post on Zillow?", *Seattle Post-Intelligencer,* September 20, 2006, http://blog.seattlepi.nwsource.com/venture/archives/106941.asp

38 St. John, Warren, "When Information Becomes T.M.I.", *New York Times,* September 10, 2006, http://www.nytimes.com/2006/09/10/fashion/10FACE.html

39 "Xanga.com to Pay $1 Million for Violating Children's Online Privacy Protection Rule", Federal Trade Commission, September 7, 2006, http://www.ftc.gov/opa/2006/09/xanga.htm

40 Digg user statistics and trends, August 2, 2006, http://duggtrends.com/stats/entry/27.aspx

41 "NAVTEQ Reports Record Second Quarter Revenue", July 26, 2006, MarketWatch, http://www.marketwatch.com/News/Story/Story.aspx?guid=%7BAF6693E8-AB56-4F61-9E4C-289048D871DF%7D&siteid=mktw&sid=1796833&symb=

42 Nanos, Brian P., "NAVTEQ on the Map", Medill News Service, August 18, 2005, http://mesh.medill.northwestern.edu/mnschicago/archives/2005/08/navteq_the_larg.html

43 Haughey, Matt, "Flickr's Creative Commons Area Back, Grown Way Over a Million Images Licensed", April 29, 2005, http://creativecommons.org/weblog/entry/5425

44 Schutzberg, Adena, "The Technology Behind Google Maps", *Directions,* February 19, 2005, http://www.directionsmag.com/article.php?article_id=760&trv=1

45 "Telcontar Unveils Framework and Fluid Maps", *Directions,* May 8, 2006, http://www.directionsmag.com/press.releases/index.php?duty=Show&id=14216

46 "Photobucket Leads Photo-sharing Sites", Hitwise, June 21, 2006,
    http://weblogs.hitwise.com/leeann-prescott/2006/06/photobucket_leads_photo_sharin.html

47 Frommer, Dan, "Your Tube, Whose Dime?", *Forbes,* April 28, 2006,
    http://www.forbes.com/intelligentinfrastructure/2006/04/27/video-youtube-myspace_cx_df_0428video.html

48 Jarin, Xeni, "TextAmerica Won't Kill Free Accounts After All", June 30, 2006,
    http://www.boingboing.net/2006/06/30/update_textamerica_w.html

49 Sullivan, Laurie, "eBay Developers Create Huge Software-As-A-Service Community", TechWeb, March 3, 2006,
    http://www.techweb.com/wire/ebiz/181500918

50 Gross, Adam, "Hello, AppExchange", January 9, 2006,
    http://blog.sforce.com/sforce/2006/01/hello_appexchan.html

51 "Using JSON with Yahoo! Web Services", Yahoo! Developer Network,
    http://developer.yahoo.com/common/json.html

52 See *http://www.programmableweb.com*

53 Service System Status, *http://status.salesforce.com*

54 Hardy, Quentin, "Why Google Loves The Little Guys", *Forbes,* Sept, 18, 2006,
    http://www.forbes.com/business/2006/09/17/mashup-search-google-tech-cz_qh_0918google.html

55 "Tactical Services: A Winning Strategy", *IT* Architect, February 1, 2006,
    http://www.itarchitect.com/shared/article/showArticle.jhtml?articleId=177100823

56 Ricadela, Aaron, "The Dark Side of SOA", *InformationWeek,* September 4, 2006
    http://www.informationweek.com/news/showArticle.jhtml?articleID=192501102&pgno=1&queryText=

57 Fried, Jason, "Getting Real, the New Book from the Makers of Basecamp", March 15, 2006,
    http://www.basecamphq.com/forum/viewtopic.php?pid=8782

58 Manjoo, Farhad, "The Next Web Revolution", Salon, August 10, 2005,
    http://dir.salon.com/story/tech/feature/2005/08/10/37signals/index.html?pn=1

59 Liedtke, Michael, "Google Upgrades Mapping Tools", *Sacramento Bee,* June 13, 2006
    http://www.sacbee.com/content/business/24hour_tech_business/story/3308241p-12188202c.html

60 MacManus, Richard, "Live.com Pushes the Limits of Users' Patience", ZDNet, April 27, 2006,
    http://blogs.zdnet.com/web2explorer/?p=168

61 Raymond, Eric S., *The Cathedral and the Bazaar,* Chapter 4, O'Reilly

62 Yahoo! Analyst Day Report, 2006,
    http://yhoo.client.shareholder.com/downloads/2006AnalystDay.pdf

63 Fried, Jason, "Don't forget there's another kind of scaling", October 8, 2004,
    http://www.37signals.com/svn/archives/000881.php

64 Songini, Marc L., "More Problems with Salesforce.com Service", February 16, 2006,
    http://www.techworld.com/applications/news/index.cfm?NewsID=5390

65 Information Technology Infrastructure Library,
    http://www.itil.co.uk

66 Anderson, Chris, *The Long Tail: Why the Future of Business Is Selling Less of More,* Hyperion

67 Anderson, Chris, "The Long Tail", *Wired,* October 2004,
    http://www.wired.com/wired/archive/12.10/tail.html

68 Anderson, Chris, *The Long Tail: Why the Future of Business is Selling Less of More,* pg. 57, Hyperion

69 Hornik, David, "Where's the Money in the Long Tail?"
    http://p6.hostingprod.com/@www.ventureblog.com/articles/indiv/2005/001227.html

70 Surowiecki, James, *The Wisdom of Crowds,* Doubleday

71 CAPTCHA is an acronym for Completely Automated Public Turing test to tell Computers and Humans Apart. See the CAPTCHA Project, Carnegie Mellon University,
    http://www.captcha.net

72 Gomes, Lee, "Many Companies Still Cling to Big Hits to Drive Earnings", *Wall Street Journal,* August 2, 2006,
    http://online.wsj.com/public/article/SB115447712983624018-0lesF4BaCaky8M_CIQ_qf11qgPA_20070802.html?mod=blogs

73 Godin, Seth, "Small Is the New Big",
    http://sethgodin.typepad.com/seths_blog/2005/06/small_is_the_ne.html

74 Stern, Allen, "Future of Web Apps—Kevin Rose", September 13, 2006,
    http://www.centernetworks.com/future-of-web-apps-kevin-rose

75 "PhotoBucket Leads Photo-sharing Sites; Flickr at #6", Hitwise, June 21, 2006
    http://weblogs.hitwise.com/leeann-prescott/2006/06/photobucket_leads_photo_sharin.html

76 Terdiman, Daniel, "Friendster Quickly Gathering Foes", *Wired,* November 23, 2003,
    http://www.wired.com/news/culture/0,1284,61150,00.html

77 Fonesca, Brian, "MySpace Makes Room with EMC, Isilon", eWeek, April 7, 2006,
    http://www.eweek.com/article2/0,1759,1947684,00.asp?kc=EWRSS03119TX1K0000594

78 Markoff, John, and Hansell, Saul, "Hiding in Plain Sight, Google Seeks More Power", *New York Times,* June 14, 2006, *http://www.nytimes.com/2006/06/14/technology/14search.html*

79 "Customer Satisfaction Index Finds Satisfaction with eCommerce", *http://www.the-dma.org/cgi/dispnewsstand?article=4486+++++*

80 Barnes & Noble book page Web 2.0 elements, including customer reviews, authorized sellers, people who bought this book also bought, and online reading groups. May 2006, *http://search.barnesandnoble.com/booksearch/isbninquiry.asp?ISBN=0307277674&z=y&cds2Pid=9481*

81 Amazon.com Community Participation Guidelines, *http://www.amazon.com/gp/help/customer/display.html?nodeId=14279631*

82 Linden, Greg; Smith, Brent; and York, Jeremy, "Amazon.com Recommendations: Item-to-Item Collaborative Filtering", *http://hugo.csie.ntu.edu.tw/~yjhsu/courses/u2010/papers/Amazon%20Recommendations.pdf*

83 "Amazon Web Services Success Story: SmugMug", Amazon.com press release, *http://www.amazon.com/b/ref=sc_fe_r_3_3435361_1/002-2459813-8946462?ie=UTF8&node=206910011&no=3435361*

84 LaMonica, Martin, "Bezos: Meet the 'Other Amazon'", CNET, September 27, 2006, *http://news.com.com/Bezos+Meet+the+other+Amazon/2100-7345_3-6097729.html*

85 The name refers to the 18th-century chess-playing machine that was actually driven by a hidden human player.

86 Kurtzman, Cliff, "Attack of the Amazons: Data Mining at Amazon.com", September 15, 2004, *http://www.adastro.com/apogee/amazon.html*

87 Nash, Kim S. "Profiles: Lessons From the Leaders in the Baseline500, Interview with Amazon.com's Werner Vogels", *Baseline,* October 19, 2005 *http://www.baselinemag.com/article2/0,1540,1872493,00.asp*

88 Amazon Honor System, *http://www.amazon.com/exec/obidos/tg/browse/-/542032/002-2524099-8268008*

89 Koman, Richard, "Stewart Butterfield on Flickr", February 4, 2005, *http://www.oreillynet.com/pub/a/network/2005/02/04/sb_flckr.html*

90 Reinventing a category whose flashbulb burnt out *http://www.fastcompany.com/fast50_05/profile/index.html?stewart_butterfield718*

91 ibid

92 ibid

93 Creative Commons, *http://creativecommons.org*

94 Haughey, Matt, "Flickr's Creative Commons Area Back, Grown Way Over a Million Images Licensed", April 29, 2005, *http://creativecommons.org/weblog/entry/5425*

95 Exchangeable Image File data, *http://www.exif.org*

96 International Press Telecommunications Council, *http://www.iptc.org*

97 Henderson, Cal, "Web Services Mash-Up", ETech 2005 Conference presentation, *http://www.iamcal.com/talks/etech2005.pps*

98 Flickr Mobile Site, *http://www.flickr.com/mob*

99 Carson Workshops, "Building Enterprise Web Apps on a Budget—How We Built Flickr", July 19, 2006, *http://www.carsonworkshops.com/dev/henderson/25AUG2005.html*

100 Henderson, Cal, *Building Scalable Web Sites,* O'Reilly, *http://www.oreilly.com/catalog/web2apps*

101 Henderson, Cal, "Taking Flickr to Gamma", Future of Web Apps Summit, *http://www.iamcal.com/talks/cal_summit_small.pdf*

102 Ozzie, Ray, "Wiring the Web", March 7, 2006, *http://rayozzie.spaces.live.com/blog/cns!FB3017FBB9B2E142!285.entry*

103 "Google Data APIs Overview", *http://code.google.com/apis/gdata*

About the Author

John Musser is the founder of ProgrammableWeb.com, the online resource for mashups, APIs, and the Web as platform. He is a Seattle-based technology consultant, writer, and teacher. During his 20-year career in software development, he has shipped five award-winning software products in three industries working with companies including Electronic Arts, Credit Suisse, MTV, and Bell Labs. He has taught at Columbia University, the University of Washington, and has written for a variety of technology publications on software development.

NOTES

NOTES

NOTES

NOTES

NOTES

web 2.0 EXPO

APRIL 15–18, 2007
MOSCONE WEST, SAN FRANCISCO
www.web2expo.com

Web 2.0 Expo is the event for the entire Web 2.0 world: the designers, developers, entrepreneurs, marketers, VCs, business strategists, and IT and web-ops managers who are building the next generation web.

Featuring a five-track conference, a full tradeshow floor, and a whole host of ways to participate, Web 2.0 Expo will be the center of gravity for this influential and innovative community.

Produced by:

CMP
United Business Media

O'REILLY